THE CORRUPT
NEW YORK CITY JUDGES

THE CORRUPT NEW YORK CITY JUDGES

BY STANLEY YALKOWSKY

In Dedication to my daughter Peree.

In Memory of my father Morris.

In Love of my mother Anna.

CONTENTS

PREFACE

Every allegation, claim, and quote in this book is true and supported by sworn affidavits, trial transcripts, and tape recorded conversations. The theme of the work is the corruption of the courts. What, if anything, can be done about what has been written, is left to the reader to decide.

DEANA

Marriage

It was September 1958, just a few days before I was to enter law school. I saw her coming out of a park by New York University. A certain angle to her face; jet-black hair flowing to her hips; bronzed brown skin; eyes black, flashing, and shining. My heart reached over to her before my body could follow.

I said, "Hello!"

She smiled. I thought perhaps she was Chinese—or Japanese. She was neither. She was a Filipina. She did not speak English very well but she did not have to. Eyes dancing, fingers fluttering—she had a language all her own: some sounds, a few words, a touch. She said something; I didn't understand, but no matter what she said, she felt for me and I for her. Her name was Deana. A story was about to begin. I accepted my role. It had been assigned to me. Everything was ready. The page was turned. It began.

We walked a little way and began to speak. While we were exchanging mere words and gestures, another activity was at work. It was a process that no one has ever been able to understand. Motions and movements, flows and exchanges of flows. Silently and quickly passing between the two of us were the mysteries and histories of our selves.

I remember to this day the exact spot I first saw her and intercepted her, right inside Washington Square Park. It was a monumental moment to me, a personal historical landmark. Nothing in life has more extranatural meaning than the chance meetings and mystical bindings that occur between man and woman. Directions change, lives unfold.

I spent weeks with Deana, maybe months, before I touched her. Finally we kissed. She kissed as if it were her first time.

But then our relationship took a more serious turn. She put a necklace of flowers around my neck, a token of love in her islands, and said to me, "I love you." I knew she did but her saying it startled me.

No one ever loved me the way she did. With her last penny she would buy me the most expensive gifts. Every thought and moment of her day was centered entirely on me. Every doodle or note she scribbled had my name. All unhappiness seemed to disappear when she appeared.

Still, I could not marry her. She was not only of a different religion, she was of a different race. I was not a martyr. If anything, I was bigoted, fiercely nationalistic, and against interracial marriage both personally and intellectually. I stopped seeing her.

I urged her to meet other boys. She refused and said she did not want to be with anyone else. But after some months she did begin to go out. I told myself I was happy for her. But I was not. My eyes became more and more watchful. One of the men she was with I positively disliked, the one she was seeing the most: Professor Fuentes, the Spanish teacher.

She seemed to be growing fond of him. I even spotted her waiting for him. I forbade her to see him. She refused. She soon had the audacity to tell me to leave her alone and let her see who she wanted. After all, I was not seeing her; and what appeared to her to be reasonable, and to anyone else reasonable, struck me as unreasonable. I argued that he was too old for her and that he was not well-intentioned. I also concluded that it was my fault that her life had taken such a bad turn. I started to become very unhappy. I began to brood. I started to watch her from a distance, unseen. My weight began to drop. I couldn't sleep, I couldn't eat. I had no idea what was wrong with me, but something was very wrong. It became clear to me. I was in love with her.

I was sick and getting sicker. I visited my mother, and told her what had happened to me. She said, "Go to her." I called Deana and nervously awaited her voice. She was not responsive. I called again. She would see me, just see me. I was aglow.

We met. I was jittery. She had a blank look. We went to a friend's apartment. We made love. It was not good. She said she felt nothing. I felt expelled and devastated. I held back tears. I returned home to my mother too dull in spirit to appraise my own damage. The phone rang that same night. It was Deana. She wanted to see me again. We would try. No promises were made. We met the next day. Her love was there. We were back, right to where we were before, in the beginning.

Deana began to visit me more and more at my Sunnyside apartment. I was still not prepared, however, to have her stay with me permanently. I still could not do it. Even though I knew I could not be without her, I just could not marry her.

But it was my decision to impregnate her. That decision allowed me to at last marry her—it would also result in our daughter, Peree.

Reverend Bragg married us. It was done. Even though we had lived together, the marriage document meant something. I vowed not to look at another woman and I meant it. I also resolved never to feel shame for her again. I scolded myself for every time I had pulled my hand from hers and for the embarrassment I felt when the eyes of others scrutinized me. I was now ready for any insult and any challenge and prepared for a life that was going to be very difficult for my newly formed interracial family.

I knew how I felt before I decided to marry Deana. I could not expect the world I was living in to feel any differently. All my resources would have to be used in some way to make up for the expected hardships that Deana and the baby she was carrying would face in the coming years.

It was time for me to study for the bar examination. In those days there was a course given known as the Sparacio Law Review Course. It was at that course that I met Howard Bushin. We became close friends and would remain friends for years to come.

Deana was doing her own studying—to become an Orthodox Jew. Together we visited a rabbi at a Queens temple. He did not want to convert Deana; no rabbi wanted to. The rabbi's facial expression pleaded with me—"Don't, Stanley, don't make me do this."

Peree was born.
Deana was not prepared for motherhood. When the baby cried, Deana would also cry and hand her to me, pleading, "What do I do?" My mother was a tremendous help. She regularly made two-hour train trips from the Bronx and helped Deana in any way she could. My father would not accompany her on these trips.

I broke my father's heart when I married Deana. He would not talk to me or look at Peree. Soon, though, he began to mellow—I could see it. When we would visit my mother, he would steal looks at Peree. His warmth and love were there for his first grandchild. He wanted to hug her so much and he wanted to talk to me and have me as his son again.

Peree was about a year old when my father began to carry her and shower her with his affection; and soon we were talking again. Slowly, but ever so certainly, my father was beginning to like Deana. My father, a man who had lived under Russian and Polish occupation as a child, who had seen Kazakhs and Asiatics in Russian cities, people who were as foreign to him as the Malay girl living with his son, was won over. Deana became his favorite daughter-in-law. They would sit for hours talking about their homelands, the natural fruits, the terrain, the people. They would laugh as my father poked fun at my mother in his usual deprecating way. For years and years after, my parents would visit us every Sunday. And on each occasion Deana gave them more respect, warmth, and hospitality than they had ever received in their lives.

Deana's studies for her conversion to Judaism were nearly completed. My harsh grimaces at the rabbi, plus Deana's charm and loveliness, overcame his resistance. A date was scheduled for Deana to appear before three rabbis dressed in long black coats. They asked her several questions, and she satisfactorily answered them. Later she went to a *mikvah*, a ritual bath, and took our daughter, Peree, who was not Jewish yet, with her. Both she and Peree were immersed in the ritual water and became "Jews." Deana and I were married again; this time in a Queens synagogue.

After failing twice, I finally passed the bar exam. I was a lawyer at last. I took an office in the Woolworth Building, on the 33rd floor. Nobody called me other than Deana and my mother. It was foolish. I had to do something. My friend Howard Bushin and I walked over to the Manhattan Criminal Court. In those days it was possible to be appointed by a judge to represent a person who was arrested and did not have a lawyer. Talking in the corridors with other lawyers, I learned that I could take money from these people. All I had to do was ask to no longer be their assigned lawyer and I could be paid by them. That is why so many lawyers were in the courtroom sitting and squirming on a long bench, smiling and laughing at the judge's jokes, hoping that the judge would choose them.

I left my office in the Woolworth Building and found a small office in one of the most decrepit areas of the Bronx, on Freeman Street, a bustling center of unemployed Puerto Ricans and blacks. It was the year John F. Kennedy was assassinated. My office was on street level. I had a big sign that said "Abogado"; a smaller sign said "Se habla Espanol," and another that said "Income tax, $2 State, $2 Federal." I was busy from the day I opened my office.

Deana was pregnant again. One day, when she was in her eighth month, she said, "Stanley, I felt a tug and a silence. I think the baby is dead." We checked with our doctor and she was right. The baby was dead. Deana delivered the dead girl a month later, on Christmas Day. To the last moment we hoped the child would be alive but she was dead. We decided to have another child right afterwards. It would become our son, Larin.

I loved Deana and treasured her, and the births of our children filled me with the greatest pleasure.

I was truly a married man. I went to work as a native hunts for food for his family. Every evening when I returned, the most carefully prepared dishes and the warmest kisses were waiting for me. And at night I was smothered with love, as she would cradle me in her arms and caress me endlessly.

Peree was five years old when she began her studies at the Akiba Jewish Academy. She learned her Hebrew studies well. Deana would bundle her up with scarves and wait with her each day on a cold corner for the bus to come to take her to school.

It was a pretty sight, Deana pregnant and pushing the carriage with Larin inside, Peree holding her hand, and I rushing to greet them.

Irina was born. I could swear that when Irina was one day old, she smiled at her mother. Irina would immediately and forever be Deana's favorite.

Criminal Courts

When I first walked into the Bronx Criminal Court building, it was a maze of activity—lawyers, bondsmen, cops, criminals, spectators; noisy halls and countless cigarette butts. I wanted to find out if I could make a living there. I tried talking to the other lawyers. Every lawyer I spoke to told me not to waste my efforts. It was clear that they did not want any more competition. Maybe they sensed that they were going to have their hands full when I arrived.

I started working in the Bronx courts by taking assignments from judges, as I did with Bushin in the Manhattan courts. It was lucrative. Every Saturday and Sunday morning I was at the court by nine A.M. My business card was on the judge's desk and I was ready for my assignments. Sometimes $100 or more was made in a day. I learned that certain crimes indicated the receipt of better fees than others. I learned that those charged with sexual crimes paid well. Perhaps they felt guilty about what they had done and wanted to overpay a lawyer as another way of punishing themselves. Whatever the reasons, the generalization was correct. The sexual offenders paid well.

The criminal courts and how each lawyer made his living were a puzzle to me, but some of the picture was clearing; assignments explained part of it. I also learned that certain types of crimes, such as gambling, were controlled in a particular way. Certain lawyers took these cases almost automatically. The arrested person often did not even know the lawyer standing beside him who was defending him.

I soon unraveled yet another secret of the courts. As the aggrieved relatives of an accused criminal came rushing into the court, they would approach lawyers for help. More often, however, it was the lawyer who approached them to offer help, and for a substantial fee. This was wonderful for me. I had no difficulty approaching strangers. I became very aggressive in the corridors of the court, approaching prospects at random.

I had seen this phenomenon many years before when I had visited the Chicago criminal courts; the lawyers there would take turns standing in front of a sign in order to block it from being seen. The sign read, "No soliciting by lawyers."

Bondsmen played a large part in the process. People would often go to a bondsman first, who would, in turn, refer a lawyer. Cops also played their part. Many would arrest a suspect and then refer him to a lawyer. It seemed soothing to the accused. It gave him a feeling of security, a feeling that he would be getting better treatment, particularly since the very person who arrested him was in a way trying to help him. The political clubs referred certain cases to certain lawyers. Lawyers who did not practice criminal law referred their clients to the ones around the Bronx court who did. And there were certain intermediaries, men of no particular description, who were friendly with certain judges and knew what lawyer to choose when something special had to be done.

With my energies now free to be unleashed, I went after clients, I was told, with a vigor never seen before. It did not take me more than a year before I had a following equal to that of the more important lawyers of Bronx County. There was much grumbling. It was rumored that I charged low fees, that I approached people knowing that they already had a lawyer, that I made promises to clients that I could not guarantee, that I was not a lawyer. None of this was true.

A new lawyer appeared at the Bronx Criminal Court. Well-dressed and tall, Steve Green had gone to good schools and came from the wealthy Long Island community of Great Neck. He didn't seem to fit. All the other lawyers were Bronx neighborhood boys. Steve Green looked like someone who should be working in a prestigious Wall Street law office. Every time he walked into a room, a restaurant, or a court, it appeared as if he had just been blown in by a great gust of wind. He seemed to be kicking off snow from his shoes, shrugging off water from his coat, sweeping back his hair. His entrances had a drama. He didn't appear, he burst in upon the scene.

For a while there was less talk about me, and the other lawyers muttered more about him. But even I began to mutter to myself about him. While his appearance was dignified, he had the same abandon as I and was wildly aggressive. I began to wait outside the court before the people could enter the building so I could get a first chance to talk to them. Once he saw what I was doing, he was on the street doing the same. He followed me and learned all my tricks. I had certain interpreters and court officers who were giving me business. He approached the same people. I now felt about him as the other lawyers felt about me—I didn't like him.

The fierce competition between the two of us for clients overwhelmed the other lawyers, who became more and more vocal with their complaints. Letters of complaint were reported to have been sent to bar associations, ethics committees, even the district attorney. Rumors circulated that I was being investigated. In fact, it was rumored that the district attorney had sent investigators with hidden tape recorders to the criminal courts to lure me into approaching them so that further facts could be accumulated to lead to my indictment and disbarment. I couldn't sleep at night.

This was no small worry. The District Attorney of Bronx County, Burton Roberts, was one of the most feared DAs in the state. But I was still at the courthouse every day.

Just when the competition between Green and me had reached explosive levels, it appeared that I finally outmaneuvered him by finding the ideal location to have my new office—right next to the Bronx Criminal Court, at street level. Now, with my new office in the best possible location, I could easily outflank him with my availability and access to clients.

I made an agreement with the landlord. But, as soon as Green heard about my move, he immediately recognized the importance of that office and, with the help of his father, who had real estate dealings with the same landlord, persuaded the landlord to let him share the office with me. So the two of us, who over the past months had been on the verge of blows and were not on speaking terms, and who were philosophically and socially so different from each other, were thrown together in a tiny office at 900 Brook Avenue.

Our little office was right next to a Greek restaurant. Before court opened each morning, the restaurant was the center of activity. The district attorneys, lawyers, judges, cops, and bondsmen all had breakfast there.

One day, while I was eating in the Greek restaurant, I was approached by a judge who insisted on knowing if I had anything against him since I never made any deals with him to help my clients. The judge was convinced that I was bribing other judges and, for some reason, did not trust him. He was actually hurt. To assure him that this was not so I bought him some neckties.

There were many other incidents of this kind. Two prominent judges demanded that I have my cases tried before them. Why judges would strive to have my cases heard by them perplexed me, but I soon learned the reason. The two judges had been so active in receiving bribes from a select group of lawyers that almost every case they heard was brought by these same lawyers and dismissed. They needed my clients to convict, so that they could show the court administration, which was involved in a survey at that time, that not everyone who appeared before them was innocent and represented by the same lawyers. This relationship between lawyers and judges was so well known that prospective clients, especially those arrested for gambling or narcotics, often would ask me, "Who's your judge?" When I told them I had none, they politely explained to me that under those circumstances, I could be of no service to them.

Corruption raged throughout the criminal courts. There were very few honest judges. Yet according to the Court of the Judiciary, which had been monitoring the conduct of judges since its creation in 1947, corrupt judges did not exist in the New York State courts.

Election Campaign

During that time I wanted to convince myself that, in addition to being financially successful, I was also capable of doing something respectable and worthwhile with my life. So, in 1965, when I was asked by the Republican party of Bronx County to run for the State Assembly, I accepted.

There were issues at stake in the campaign at that time that I did not dare to discuss. Court corruption was not something I wanted to stress. Not while I was soliciting clients in the courts.

John Lindsay, however, the Republican mayoral candidate, said that if he was elected, he would find out once and for all if judgeships were being bought. Of course judgeships were being purchased. In 1960 the Russell Sage Foundation, one of the oldest and most respected social science research foundations in the nation, after making a study of the topic, concluded in its findings that two years' salary was the "going rate" for judgeships, paid in the form of a contribution to party campaign funds.

I bought a loudspeaker and attached it to my car. My campaign was ready to begin. I drove in and out of the Bronx streets, bellowing long speeches on all sorts of diverse subjects. Scarcely anyone opened their windows to listen to what I had to say.

While campaigning, I noticed that the major candidates were putting their posters almost everywhere, I decided to make that my main objective; it was a way to advertise myself as a lawyer (which at the time was not permitted) and at the same time suggest to my clients that I must be very important to be a candidate for elective office. My posters with my photographs were soon located in as many places as the most important candidates.

The more established of them started to complain and retaliate. They began covering my posters with theirs. I counterattacked by re-covering their posters. It was open warfare. Myself against all the other candidates; not to win the election (I had no chance of winning, and didn't win), but just to post signs.

Moving to Scarsdale

At the time most professionals—lawyers, doctors, and accountants—fled to the suburbs, as white communities formed and grew in a circular pattern around the city of New York. The pressure upon Deana and me to move was enormous. Finally I succumbed, and purchased an expensive home in Scarsdale.

I calculated that I was now part of that small percentage of men of great achievement, able to live, as I thought, in the most desirable community in the world. Bushin soon followed, moving to Scarsdale as well.

Only months after we moved, Risah was born. She was delivered on December 25, 1969—Christmas Day, the same day that our second daughter had been delivered dead.

Scarsdale was beautiful. My house was beautiful. We had four bedrooms, three bathrooms, two cars, and a lawn that resembled a park. The schools were beautiful. Even the stores in town were beautiful. I had wealth. I had Deana. I had four children.

* * *

The venetian blinds were drawn, but not tightly. My feet were bare as I stood naked by the glass door of my street-level office. I could hear people talking outside on the street. The mention of my name would startle me from my reverie. "Have you seen Stanley? His office has been closed for months." I could recognize their voices. They were lawyers I had worked with and had known for years. "What happened to him? He had a tremendous practice and made a fortune buying and selling gold." "He is a member of the Commodity Exchange." "He owns apartment houses, but his tenants can't find him." Even though they were talking about me and their words were clearly audible, I often lost contact with their conversation and was more content to contemplate the peculiar configuration of my toes. "He sleeps in the office. I see people knocking on his door, but he never answers it." I was still staring at my toes when I became aware of their silence. I peeked through the slot and saw them motioning to one another, and grimacing comically. They were pointing to my toes, which were partially visible to them. I could see other lawyers being beckoned over. They were laughing. "That's his feet!" It was April 1978.

FIRST
TRIAL

Napolitano

The trial of Stanley Yalkowsky versus Deana Sayoc Yalkowsky began on February 17, 1981, in Westchester County Supreme Court at 111 Grove Street, the White Plains courthouse.

I had sued Deana for divorce; my claim was that she had an adulterous relationship with Americo Napolitano, a gardening contractor who owned the Greenlawn Landscaping Company. Napolitano denied the relationship.

My attorney, Richard Friedman, called Napolitano to the stand as the first witness. Over the years Friedman had questioned Napolitano on several prior occasions. Napolitano had been represented during these proceedings by Benjamin Shedler, the same lawyer who was now representing Deana.

Friedman asked, "Mr. Napolitano, in 1978 to 1979 was Mrs. Yalkowsky employed by Greenlawn?"

Napolitano replied, "No, she was not carried as an employee. She was not an employee."

Napolitano, in affidavit after affidavit, swore that Deana had no relationship with him, financial, romantic, or otherwise. Benjamin Shedler, who prepared those affidavits, also insisted that Deana was not involved, financially or romantically, with Napolitano, claiming that my belief in the existence of this relationship was paranoid.

Friedman was now ready to proceed with proofs that checks issued to Jhana Yalkowsky or to Jhana Sayoc (her maiden name) were actually received by Deana from Napolitano, despite his claims that they were not. A W-2 form and several payroll checks of Greenlawn Landscaping Co., Inc., bearing Jhana Yalkowsky's name were presented to Judge Walsh.

But Napolitano still maintained that Deana did not receive these checks. He claimed that he had forged her signature to them and cashed them, without her knowledge.

Napolitano had an important reason for maintaining this position. If Deana's destitution and lack of assets could be established, by showing that she had not been paid by his Greenlawn Landscaping corporation and that she had no bank accounts, she could be assured of receiving substantial support payments from me.

Friedman then introduced a photostat of an application for a safety deposit box at the National Bank of North America, dated August 1977, bearing Napolitano's and Jhana Sayoc's signatures.

Shedler intervened: "If Your Honor pleases, I object to this unless there is some proof that Jhana Sayoc or Yalkowsky signed it."

Walsh more than agreed with Shedler, saying, "Quite to the contrary. He said she didn't sign. He signed it. The jury has heard that."

Walsh ended that day's testimony by instructing the jurors to refrain from discussing the case among themselves. We were all instructed to return to the Westchester courthouse the next morning when Mr. Napolitano would continue with his testimony.

Friedman, his assistant, Curt Meltzer, and I packed our many documents and carried them to the car, a ritual we followed each day.

During the drives to and from court, Friedman, who had long since been divorced, and I spoke disparagingly of life with women, while Meltzer, a thickly bearded young man, spoke in glowing terms of his ideal marriage. Meltzer thought, perhaps quite rightfully, that Friedman and I were mistaken failures, who had lost the most important battle of our lives and covered our losses with unhappy reproaches of women.

Friedman, for his part, thought little of Meltzer, and even less of me, especially when he realized that I was serious when I told him I would not give one penny to a judge to fix a case, even if it would save me hundreds of thousands of dollars. This made little sense to Friedman. While Friedman could understand my wanting to protect myself from a lawyer pocketing money that was supposed to go to a judge, he could not understand how I could possibly be opposed to paying a judge for a favorable result, especially if I knew that the judge would actually be receiving the money.

Friedman also wondered why I had hired him, if I was so virtuous, when I must have known that he was a lawyer who had bribed numerous judges. This was not something Friedman avoided discussing. Lawyers who could bribe judges were honored and wanted this ability of theirs known. It was the most impressive achievement to encourage their recruitment that they could display.

There was another reason why Friedman's services were so sought after. He had recently been investigated by Maurice Nadjari, one of the most feared Special Prosecutors to ever investigate corruption in the New York City courts. Friedman survived Nadjari's investigation. This was no small accomplishment. It meant to knowledgeable litigants that Friedman had influence that reached into the highest courts.

I explained to Friedman that while I knew of his ability to influence judges, I hired him because he was a good lawyer and for no other reason.

The trial resumed on February 19, 1981. Napolitano, when questioned, referred to his lawyer, Mr. Shedler, as Judge Shedler, saying, "I know him as a judge. I don't know if he still is." When Friedman asked, "Where was he a judge, do you know?" Walsh interjected, "Let's get off this subject. I am going to advise the jury that as far as we are concerned in this courthouse the only judge is the judge that is sitting in this courtroom."

Walsh was wise to interrupt the questioning. He knew the mentality of men like Shedler. The courts were filled with lawyers who had once been judges, even for the shortest time, who called themselves "judges" for the rest of their lives. Having a former judge as a lawyer was unquestionably a valuable possession, so valuable that the largest and wealthiest law firms in the city, instead of crudely boasting of their influence, often display on their stationery the retired judges who are members of their firm so that prospective clients could be subtly told which segment of the judiciary could be reached by them.

Friedman presented another account in Napolitano's and Deana's names at the National Bank of North America. But Shedler responded, saying, "There seem to be two signatures on this card."

Napolitano then answered, "I signed both of them."

Shedler then stated, "With that reservation, Judge, I have no objection to it going into evidence."

Friedman then showed Napolitano yet another account, this one maintained at the Scarsdale National Bank in the name of the Greenlawn Landscaping Company. This account had Americo Napolitano designated as secretary treasurer and Jhana Sayoc as president. It had monthly balances, often in excess of $100,000. Shedler and Walsh again made certain that the evidence of this account could be seen by the jury only if they were to understand that it was Napolitano's claim that he signed both names and that Deana did not sign her own name.

Friedman then attempted to show the jury Napolitano's pay-roll records. Friedman thought that there was still the possibility that Judge Walsh was not corrupt but just limited intellectually, and that even in his limited capacity he would soon respond to the evidence.

Walsh stopped Friedman, saying, "I don't see what relevance they have."

Friedman answered, "I'll tell you what they are, Judge. The witness denied that this lady was actually employed by the business. He says that she is not an employee—this is the payroll stub that shows the ordinary course of business by the accountant and that's what I want to question him on."

Walsh replied, "I don't care about that—it doesn't prove anything with respect to her."

Friedman protested, "It shows that they were issued to her."

Walsh concluded, "I am not going to take it."

Napolitano's Greenlawn Landscaping Company employee records, which he admitted he prepared for his accountant, listing Jhana Yalkowsky as a salaried employee earning $300 per week, were excluded by Judge Walsh as evidence that Deana worked for Greenlawn Landscaping Company. At that point Friedman exchanged a knowing glance with me.

Napolitano was then questioned about an application form for a Visa credit card that he filled out for Deana Yalkowsky. Shedler was expecting Napolitano once again to deny that Deana had signed this document, and once again say that he had forged her name. Napolitano, however, disappointed Shedler. This time he answered, "I am not sure."

Shedler, only momentarily shaken, protested, "There is no proof that it was signed by Mrs. Yalkowsky." Walsh said the same.

But Napolitano was not able to go as far as Walsh and Shedler were willing to go. Napolitano explained, "She came to me to fill it out to establish credit in order to have a phone put back in her home, and I helped her with that and in that case she did sign it."

Walsh then said, "We are getting into argument. We don't want to get into procedures of credit card numbers now. Let's stay on the issue."

But there was no argument. There was no talk about credit card numbers. We were on the issue. Deana simply filled out an application for a Visa card, declared she was an employee of Greenlawn Landscaping Company earning $300 per week, listed her Social Security number, and signed the application. And Napolitano confirmed that she had signed it. The Visa card application was now in Walsh's hands and he was looking at it. Walsh made certain that there were no further discussions concerning that Visa card application.

The questioning of Napolitano shifted to a document he used to change the beneficiary of his life insurance policy. The document was dated September 30, 1976; the witness signing the document was Jhana Sayoc.

Friedman questioned Napolitano about Deana's signature on that document, asking, "Did Mrs. Yalkowsky, under her name Jhana Sayoc, sign this in front of the notary public who put her stamp on these papers?"

Napolitano replied, "No, I signed it."

Friedman then asked, "You are saying that the notary public put that stamp, signed her name here, even though you signed it?"

At this point, Shedler alarmed, intervened, "How is this material in this case?"

Friedman replied, "This witness has said that he signed it in front of a notary public."

Walsh responded, "Only as an officer of the corporation, not as a beneficiary of the policy."

Shedler, confident that Walsh had sufficiently confused the jury by his diversionary remarks into believing that a technical legal question was being debated before them rather than a travesty committed upon them, added, "If it is limited to that purpose, sir, I have no objection."

The notary, Louise Mole, appeared. The most important outcome of her testimony was the actions of Judge Walsh. When Friedman asked Louise Mole, "Madam, in your experience as a notary public of the State of New York have you ever notarized a signature on a document where the person whose name you were asked to witness was not present before you at the time?" Before Louise Mole could answer, Walsh intervened, saying, "That wouldn't prove anything."

Friedman then called to the witness stand Betty Jean Solomon, the Assistant Branch Manager of the National Bank of Westchester.

Friedman, pointing to Deana, asked Mrs. Solomon, "Do you remember the date it was that you first saw her?"

Betty Jean Solomon quickly replied, "The first time I saw her was when I opened a joint account for her and Mr. Napolitano."

Friedman, further questioned Mrs. Solomon about Deana's signature card at the bank, asking "Did she sign the card in your presence?"

Mrs. Solomon replied, "Yes."

Friedman then discussed with Mrs. Solomon a safety deposit box Deana and Napolitano maintained at that bank, asking her, "Do you have any recollection of the lady, Jhana Sayoc, going into the box?"

Mrs. Solomon replied, "Yes, I recall two times."

Walsh then interjected, "Look, Mr. Friedman, are you finished?" Friedman had little choice but to say, "I'm finished."

The next witness questioned by Friedman was Viola Amarosa, who testified that she was an assistant manager at the National Bank of North America and had been employed there for fifteen years. Friedman showed her a document used for the renting of a safety deposit box at her bank. Viola Amarosa confirmed that the document was signed by Jhana Sayoc, who was listed as "vice-pres" of Greenlawn Landscaping Company.

Friedman asked Viola Amarosa, "And can you look around this courtroom now and tell us whether or not you recognize the person who signed as Jhana Sayoc?"

Amarosa replied, "Yes."

Friedman continued, "Will you point out that person to us, please?"

Viola Amarosa pointed her finger directly at Deana and said, "The young lady straight ahead."

A childlike, bursting, happy smile covered Deana's face; it was absolutely joyous in its expression. It was not in any way feigned. It was so inappropriate to the situation that the jurors were bewildered. Why was Deana smiling so happily? An accused, when identified, is not normally overjoyed. These unrelated responses, coming at the most inappropriate moments, were perplexing.

Friedman continued, "Is it your testimony, Madam, that at the time this card was signed, that the lady you identified signed it in your presence?"

Amarosa replied, "Yes."

Friedman then called Deana Yalkowsky to the witness stand. Friedman asked Deana, "You've been here in court each day as this trial has progressed, is that correct?" Deana replied, "Yes, Mr. Friedman." Deana rarely missed a minute; she was first to arrive and last to leave.

Friedman proceeded to ask Deana about Napolitano's previous testimony that he issued several Greenlawn Landscaping Company salary checks to her. Friedman, referring to one of these checks, asked Deana if she had endorsed it. Before Deana could answer it was apparent that Shedler was shaking his head up and down, urging Deana to admit, this time, that she did sign the check. Friedman objected, and said, "Mr. Shedler, would you please not nod your head to the witness." Walsh scolded Friedman, exclaiming, "He didn't, I said that he didn't and I was watching the two of you. You have been doing the frowning and not him and I resent your criticizing comment."

If anything made the jury question the integrity of Judge Walsh, it was this very incident. They observed Shedler. It was not a question of maybe or maybe not. Shedler was directing the answer, and he had good reason to do so. Shedler, and even Walsh, had repeatedly presented the argument that Deana did not receive any of the Greenlawn Landscaping Company checks. In this instance, however, it was impossible for Deana to deny having received several of the Greenlawn Landscaping Company salary checks. The checks were before the jury. If Shedler wanted different answers from Deana, it was necessary for him to direct her. Deana had denied receipt of these checks on too many occasions.

Friedman, continuing his cross-examination of Deana, asked, "Mrs. Yalkowsky, isn't it a fact that in October of 1974 you caused to be opened a joint account with your mother, Severina Sayoc, at the People's Bank in New Rochelle?"

Deana answered, "I had forgotten about that."

Friedman pressed, "In 1980, didn't you draw out of that account $3,297.35 from passbook number H10118?"

Deana replied, "My mother is from the Philippines."

Walsh, who thought that Deana's answer could be useful, interjected, "Let's get it straight. She keeps on saying 'her mother.' Did you take it out or did your mother take it out?"

Deana who had never said nor suggested that her mother withdrew the money, saw what Walsh wanted and proceeded to accommodate him. She answered, "My mother took it out."

But when Friedman asked her the same question again, Deana clarified, "My mother was with me."

Walsh's suggestion that it was Deana's mother who took the money out was reduced to Deana admitting that it was she who took the money out and signed her name and that her mother had simply accompanied her to the bank.

I was the next witness to be called by Mr. Friedman. I testified that I was forty-six years old and had married Deana twenty years earlier. Friedman asked, "And what is your profession?" I replied, "I'm a lawyer. I used to practice criminal law."

Practicing criminal law in the Bronx was the way I had supported my family in our early years together. Yet I was every bit as much a criminal as the clients I represented. I took as much money as I could from them, believing that this was part of their punishment.

I and my fellow attorneys thought that this was our right and we all looked with respect and admiration at the lawyers among us who were able to be paid the most for doing the least. The lawyers who could accomplish this feat in the most outlandish manner were applauded. Our worst glares of scorn and contempt were reserved for those of us that were paid small fees by clients who could easily have afforded to pay substantial fees. This was considered an unforgivable misjudgment. My fellow lawyers and I enjoyed the larceny as we competed in our own life of crime, stealing from criminals and their families.

There was no such accomplishment as legal skills. If a lawyer had legal skill, there was scarcely a judge to be found in the criminal courts who would understand him. Most of the judges sitting in the criminal courts were unsuccessful lawyers who had spent years hanging around the backrooms of their political clubs until they accumulated enough money to buy their judgeship.

The Criminal Court judges were so incompetent and their decisions so embarassing that in late 1963 the Administrative Judge, John Murtagh, directed them to discontinue issuing written opinions.

Most of those I represented were guilty; and I needed to know they were guilty and I wanted them to be guilty, so if they were found guilty I could be at peace with myself. Only the hardest of our fraternity of criminal lawyers could live with the innocent imprisoned. I, and most others, could not. Someone who I thought was truly innocent, and yet who was in danger of imprisonment, I could not represent.

Practicing criminal law was not pleasant. Cruelty and misery was expected at every turn. I longed for the day when I no longer had to see the criminal courts again. In fact, it was a minor case, almost a meaningless one, that confirmed my determination to leave the field.

Roy Hashimoto was arrested. It was his first arrest. He was absolutely innocent, without question. What is more, the laws of the court provided that since the nature of the charges brought against him were so minor, and because he was a youth, his innocence be automatically found, under any circumstances.

I made an appointment with Roy's father. He was a frail looking man, a remnant of that small community of Japanese-Americans from California who had known injustice. I promised Mr. Hashimoto that I would save his son from having a criminal record. I presented myself as confident, knowledgeable, and extremely influential. My fee was exorbitant. Mr. Hashimoto gave me a small retainer. Anything I received was more than I deserved. Yet to Mr. Hashimoto, I looked official. I wore a suit, carried a business card identifying myself as an attorney at law, and was able to stand up in a court and say words to a judge and have a judge say words back to me. Mr. Hashimoto trusted me. He was so thankful for what I did for his son. I did nothing for his son; I only knew the procedures. Most clients never paid another penny once a case was over. Not Mr. Hashimoto—he insisted on paying me every penny. Week after week, for over a year, he came to my office to bring me a small payment, bowing in his traditional Japanese style and thanking me profusely. His decency and the trust he placed in me more than anything else hastened my departure from the practice of criminal law.

Friedman asked, "In the early years of your marriage to Mrs. Yalkowsky, where did you live?" I answered, "When we first married, we moved to a one-room apartment in Sunnyside, in kind of a poor area, and we set up house over there the first year of our marriage..."

This was in 1962. I had married a dark Oriental, a Filipina. Better housing was available, but not for blacks and Puerto Ricans. My wife fell into that category. It was a time of great unrest. Middle-class neighborhoods were struggling to fortify and defend their existence. An intruder from another race could cause a building to be emptied almost overnight of all its white inhabitants.

I understood the fears of the landlord. His investment in his building was in jeopardy. I had little choice of where to live. Even in run-down Sunnyside, in an undesirable building, I had to visit the landlord alone, and hope he would assume that the woman living with me was white since I was white, or I would not have been able to get an apartment even there.

I continued, "and I did something that was a little uncharacteristic at the time, in the neighborhood. I gave my wife a maid and it was a little peculiar."

Walsh interjected, "You employed a maid. You don't give a wife a maid."

The only motive I could think of for these interjections by Judge Walsh was his desire to let every member of the jury know that he did not like me. And Walsh's feelings were important. A judge's dislike for a litigant, whatever his reasons, does not pass unnoticed. A juror can recognize these feelings, and can only speculate to himself that it must be for a very good and knowledgeable reason; otherwise a judge would never be so openly hostile and biased toward a litigant appearing before him.

Friedman asked me to describe Deana's first years in Scarsdale. I answered, "I noticed that there were changes in her relationship to me, about six months after we moved to Scarsdale, I remember one time I was sick, and I was hoping that she would give me tea and take care of me while I was sick. And she said, 'I'm busy.' She left and she was gone much of the day, and I noticed, to myself, I made a mental note things are not quite the same, but I realized that we had gone a long way. We had four children, and it wasn't something that was going to change my relationship with my wife."

But it was so important. Before we moved to Scarsdale, my having a cold or not feeling well would have brought tears to her eyes. Then, she would have nursed me every minute of my illness.

I testified further. "In 1972 we had some trouble with our driveway and I mentioned to my wife, if she could get somebody to do the driveway, and she said she knew somebody who was very good, and that he would do the driveway, and that was Mr. Napolitano—he did my driveway, and that was the time I met him, and I may have said two words to him and given him a check for the work he had done."

The only recollection I had of that meeting was that somehow Napolitano wanted to let me know he was not just a simple laborer, that he read books and had a larger vocabulary than I might expect.

I continued. "Somewhere around 1974 I saw him coming out of my house, when I came home one day in the afternoon. I never came home in the afternoon and I happened to come home. I just nodded to him, and I asked my wife, 'Well, what's Mr. Napolitano doing over here?' 'Oh, he just delivered me a plant,' was her reply." I testified further, "That is my only contact with him, Napolitano, that I can recall. Until his name came into the picture on January 20th."

I added, "The other things that I noticed were, she was taking five, six, seven, eight showers a day. Enormous amounts of showers. She was always a very clean woman but not to that point."

I tried to describe what I thought was self-evident. I tried to explain to Judge Walsh and the jury what the factors were that led to my belief that my wife was unfaithful. Someone who normally took one or two showers a day was now taking seven or eight showers a day. This was a significant clue.

I explained further. "She would always be coming home with a package from Bonwit Teller or Lord and Taylor. One time, out of curiosity and suspicion, plain and simple, I looked in the trunk of her car. She had boxes, all sorts of boxes from different department stores, and I noticed the next day or the following day, she would come in with one of those boxes, so she had prepared several boxes, several items and gifts from various department stores and was taking them in each day separately, showing where she had been and what she did. My suspicion was now more than a suspicion."

Friedman, moving along, asked, "And will you take us into 1978, sir, particularly into January?"

I narrated, "On January 20th, I guess it would be January 19th, at night, my suspicions were very strong, and I said, 'Deana are you having an affair with someone?'"

No matter how suspicious I was, I still hoped to hear her say something that could evaporate the dark cloud of gloom that was hanging over us. I believed she was involved with someone. Sense and common sense compelled this belief, but then again I didn't believe she was involved. She had always proven me wrong, always shamed my doubts. I hoped for confirmation of her loyalty and love. I wanted to be the jealous husband, wrongfully accusing his faithful wife; I wanted to be wrong.

I continued, "And she started to cry and said, 'After all these years, you could dare ask a question like that?' And I was hoping, maybe I was very foolish?"

Walsh at that moment interjected, "We aren't asking you what you thought. We're asking what was said."

I replied, "She said, 'No, I'm not having an affair.' And we went to bed that night."

I remember as I lay in bed with her beside me, her leg between mine, her cry. She cried. But her cry was not that of someone hurt by my accusation. It was a wail. The cry said, "Stanley, I wronged you."

I continued with my testimony. "And at night, I asked her again. 'Are you having an affair, I know you are having an affair,' and she denied it again, and then, that morning, I asked her, 'Are you having an affair?' I pressed it once more, and she said, 'Yes, do you know with whom?' And I just stayed blank. I had no idea who it was. She said, 'It is with Mr. Napolitano.'"

I continued, "When she said that, it was as if I knew everything."

Walsh interrupted, "We aren't asking you what you thought."

I don't know if there was any thought; there was knowledge. I knew everything. Every man knows everything. It is within us from the beginning. This is our fate: what we fear, we receive. Our worst nightmare—the infidelity and disloyalty of our women—is upon us. The fear is what keeps us with our women. It binds and tapes us to them. The realization that infidelity has occurred tears us apart. The threat is the sustenance of love. The actuality, the ending. Love of another man! In one second a depth of understanding crashed through me. I knew she hated me; I knew she stole from me; I knew she had turned the children from me. I knew she had been in love with Napolitano for many years. But even before these thoughts raced through my mind, I was on the floor.

My testimony continued. "I fell apart. I fell down. I cried. I rolled on the rug. I bit the rug. I foamed from my mouth. I just completely fell apart."

Walsh responded, "You're dramatizing. I'm going to tell the jury, that is not evidence."

Friedman then asked, "Tell us what happened between you and her after January 20th."

On January 20, 1978, I stopped everything; there would be no more business. I had fortunes invested in commodities. I owned buildings with tenants clamoring for services. I had antique dealers calling me to sell their wares. I had clients with cases. I stopped it all. Everything stopped; everything was meaningless. My whole life and everything I had thought was so important lost all meaning to me in one night. Everything was taken away and belonged away: the paintings on the wall, the furniture, the beautiful lawn; the houses and people around me, the schools my children attended, the work I did. On January 20, 1978, all ventures were terminated, not to begin again.

It had never snowed like it did the week of January 20, 1978. We were virtually trapped, she and I, to endless screeching revelations and exposures, and hour after hour of talk, sleepless, relentless talk, and love. Yes, love. Bizarre, twisted love. I yearned for her and wanted her again and again. Not since we were married was she so appealing and desirable to me. She knew, though, she knew this yearning would also pass.

She saw the world. She saw its inner side. I saw only the outside. Now she showed me the inside, and I was testing her patience and her anger, because I could not see. She would scream at me, "You can't see!" I didn't know what she was talking about; I couldn't understand her. I saw her as a sensuous little darling whose heart had been stolen by a Don Juan, a womanizer, who preyed on weak women, tempting them while their husbands toiled to give them a better life. She looked at me as if I were crazy and screamed, "You are all wrong!" She called Napolitano a nice man and just an instrument for her, not an instrument for sex, but an instrument. I did not understand and she screamed again, "You don't understand."

By instinct I knew a great deal. Missing money could now be explained. I testified, "I said, 'Deana, we have fired a lot of maids because we had thought that they had taken money. There has been a lot of money missing. Did you give money to Mr. Napolitano?' She said, 'Yes, he needed it. He needed the money very badly.'"

Then one night we were lying in bed, side by side. My hands were moving. I watched my hands. I actually hit her while she was asleep. She awoke, whimpering, and crawling desperately, like a beetle, for her life. She fell from the bed and slid into the closet, pleading as I followed her. She expected to die. I was not thinking of her death. I just wanted to batter her head with my fists, hard; I was aiming at her skull. I could not stop what I was doing, and I would not have stopped, had it not been for Peree, who, having heard her mother's screams, ran up the stairs to aid her mother.

Peree saved her mother's life. She rushed into our room and blanketed her mother with her body. It was the only way to stop me, it was as if I was in a trance. Had Peree reacted in any other way, it would have been too late.

* * *

Deana insisted we visit a lawyer named Max Block, Jr. She said it was absolutely necessary we see this particular lawyer. Deana told me that Max Block was referred to her by a neighbor whose name she did not recall. Her urgency and persuasiveness concerning the meeting was irresistible. I was so weak and broken that I allowed Deana to lead me to Block's office without protesting. I did not even ask Block why I was in his office. It was an incident that had to happen. Block urged that Deana and I remain together. The nerve of such a suggestion! The weirdness of such a meeting! Yet something about Max Block, Jr., made me conclude that, of the characters I was to meet along my journey, he would be most meaningful.

Soon Deana decided that I should not live in the house any longer. After all, I was a danger; I had beaten her. I found this decision very painful. I was attached to the house, to her, to the family. It was my only life. I lingered, I found myself begging her to let me stay.

I testified: "She would tell me to go, I guess you know, when I would come home I was distraught, and she didn't want me around, and I lived in the office, and I kept the office door closed, and I would go out at night to get food and that is the life I led. I slept in my office. I had a cot there." From February to June of 1978, I lived, most of the time, in my office across the street from the Bronx Criminal Court.

Gold and Silver

Friedman moved to another area in his questioning. He asked, "Would you tell us the circumstances under which jewelry was bought for your wife?"

I explained, "I was a commodity trader and also I dealt in antiques, so I would travel to different countries and I would get scrap gold and scrap silver and bring it home, and melt it and sell it on the Commodity Exchange or sell it to the refineries. Before I sold anything, I let her look at the jewelry, to see which she would like for herself, and whatever she wanted for herself, was hers."

Friedman continued, "And these trips that you took, did you take these trips by yourself or together with your wife?"

I answered, "I went on my own on most of these silver-and-gold-gathering journeys."

My trips were frenzied, I was searching for treasure. I would be sweating in a jungle one day, and the next be freezing in a New York City taxicab. The trips were as compulsive and adventurous as anything I had ever done; they bordered on the suicidal. I was in constant danger; in my own modern way I was searching for El Dorado. I would let myself go wherever I was taken.

How did these adventures begin? On November 20, 1973, I took Deana and the children to Miami for a vacation. We arrived at Miami Airport in the early afternoon. As we were beginning our walk to the car rental service, I glanced at a flight time schedule on one of the walls of the airport. There was a departure for Panama. I told Deana to take the children by taxi to a Miami Beach hotel, that I must go to Panama and would meet her later. I gave no explanation. Without notice, without plan, without the vaguest idea of ever going to Panama,

I was on my way there, not knowing why I was going. There was also no protest, not even a comment by Deana then or ever again about that trip.

I arrived in Panama City. I walked along its main street. The plane also stopped briefly in Guatemala. The next day I was back in Miami. But something had happened. Something about my stop in Guatemala for what could have been no more than an hour made me want to go back there. And when I did, I received a grand surprise. Their coin, the *quetzal*, which was approximately equal in size and monetary exchange to our dollar, was made of 72 percent silver and was worth, at the time, at least double our coins in value. All I had to do was to exchange my United States currency for the Guatemalan coins. I went wild. I would meet bus drivers at the end of their routes in Guatemala City; I was paying 10 percent above the going rate. Word spread: the American was giving eleven American dollars for ten dollars in silver quetzal coins. In spite of my bad back, and exhaustion from the high altitude, I lugged heavy bags filled with coins. I hired young Indians to help me carry them. I must have been an odd sight, roaming a Central American city, followed by a train of Indian helpers carrying my bags and boxes of coins.

I was not the only one interested in gold and silver and treasure; I had competitors, and they were not happy with me. The new buying methods I created were not appreciated by the established silver and coin dealers from San Antonio and New Orleans, who had been doing business in Central America for years before I arrived. For my part, I saw no difference in what I was doing in Central America from what I had done in the criminal courts in the Bronx. Only now I was hustling in the streets of Guatemala, rather than the corridors of the Bronx Criminal Court.

It was a legitimate business venture—the gold and silver I was importing into the States were brought in in a perfectly legal manner; however, taking the precious metals out of Guatemala was another story. Whether it was legal or not was never made clear. One official would declare it was perfectly legal; another official would offer a totally different opinion. I could not afford to put that issue to question. It could take months or years to be resolved.

During one of my many visits to Guatemala I received an important message; it read, "Contact Alfredo Machon of El Salvador who has 50,000 ounces of plata." All appointments were postponed and I was on my way to El Salvador. There I met a most interesting and unusual man.

Machon was younger than I, with almost shoulder-length black hair and enormous black eyes. His features were European—Spanish, I would logically have guessed. After early doubts and suspicions were overcome, we became trusting and lasting friends.

Machon was more important to me than any other contact I made in Central America. In the months that followed, hundreds of thousands of ounces of silver in coins and ingots would be shipped by Machon to me.

In March of 1974, shipments from Guatemala stopped. What I had feared had happened: my silver had been seized at the airport by the Guatemalan government.

I then devised a plan to have my coins returned to me in a manner that earned me the highest respect of my Guatemalan friends. From my office in the Bronx, I convinced the Guatemalan customs agents that the calls they were receiving were directly from the official government offices of the United States and not from me, and that the seized merchandise must be released immediately by orders of the United States Government. The seized merchandise was released. I must have looked to my Central American friends like a man of the most mysterious connections.

The victory of having my goods released while others had had theirs seized permitted me to import yet larger shipments of silver from Guatemala. Rumors and gossip, as a result, circulated about the international influence I supposedly had. I did not discourage rumors: they were my security. I referred only to "my people"—a nebulous phrase that could mean anything. I wanted it only to mean that there would be retaliation if harm were to come to me.

My travels also took me to the Philippines, where, in June of 1974, I visited the island that had given me my beautiful wife. Deana accompanied me on this trip.

Before we boarded the plane to cross the Pacific, Deana and I stayed for a night at a San Francisco hotel. We made love. The movements of her body were unlike what they had ever been before; she had given me a message that I was unable to understand.

I loved Manila. A crowded street in Manila was like nothing I had experienced before: floods in the middle of the city; electric failures, angry encounters, chickens and dogs and cats. And it was hot, burning hot and dirty.

I was stared at; I looked different and they let me know it. They ran to look at me. The sun had baked my face to red. I stared back. I saw many fascinating bulgy-eyed Malay faces.

The Philippines was a treasure chest. Antiques and jewels and precious metals were to be found there at bargain prices. For my purposes it had everything I could ever dream of. But it was an uncomfortable country. I could open the door of my hotel room and find someone standing silently outside, and open it again hours later and still find the same stranger there.

I had arranged to meet Lita Tan, with whom I had corresponded before I arrived in the Philippines. Lita was an extremely successful and wealthy businesswoman. Nonetheless, despite her riches, she lived modestly in a simple apartment, one flight above her jewelry store on Sales Street, one of the most dangerous streets in Old Manila.

Lita, however, was fully protected. Bodyguards and family members patrolled her street, watching over her. She was a leader without politics. People came to her to buy, to sell, and to seek advice. She was so respected that she could, at any time interrupt a business meeting to discuss a poor Filipino's problems—or play with her child—without offending the one with whom she was engaged in conversation.

Lita's home in a way reminded me very much of my own. Seated on the floor were several trusted members of her family, counting and rolling coins and packaging and weighing them. Peree, Larin, and I would do the same in our own home, where we would count and separate the coins, taking out the rare numismatic ones while leaving the rest to be melted.

The Philippine trip turned out a surprising success. I had visited my wife's land of birth and had seen Deana's father and family. I had met Deana's sister Vicky, who was married to the highly promising young politician Manuel Benedicto. I had been to a most unusual country and had found a new source of supply for my ever-increasing quest for precious metals. We left the Philippines.

Arrangements were made for vast shipments of silver. Everything went wrong, although everything I did was absolutely legal. Importation and exportation of silver and gold were legal both in the United States and in the Philippines. Nevertheless, Lita Tan was arrested, and the silver I had purchased from her was confiscated.

A series of frightening and intriguing events followed, which were to include Lita Tan's trial in the Philippines and a great deal of attention called to me. Fortunately, nobody went to jail, and, finally, several months later, after the Philippine government declared my venture absolutely legal, I received about 20 percent of my seized coins. Manuel Benedicto, Deana's brother-in-law, acted in my behalf and was instrumental in obtaining the release of my coins. Although I truly loved the Philippines, I had no desire to ever go back there again.

In the months that followed my return from the Philippines, I lost hundreds of thousands of dollars trading silver on the Commodity Exchange. In order to recover my losses, I had to find new countries to import silver from.

Once again I set off on my travels. In November 1974 I found myself in the jewelry district of Lima, Peru. There the jewelers talked about a man named Machtinger. Machtinger, I was told, could do wonders with coins, currency, and precious metals. Originally from Argentina, he had fled to Peru just before local Argentine authorities were about to arrest him for illegal smuggling and currency transactions. In Peru, Machtinger's dealings were also noted by the authorities, but again, just before he was to be arrested, he fled, leaving his wife and five children behind. In their stead, he took with him a young Peruvian girlfriend. I was told that

Machtinger was living in Panama City, but no one knew where.

I found him: he lived right across the street from the main hotel in Panama City. He was indeed everything that had been described to me: he cursed, he gambled, and, though over seventy years of age, his head still revolved at the passing of a pretty girl.

There had been no exaggeration—Machtinger could do wonders. He supplied the jewelers of Panama with precious metals and diamonds from his warehouse in the Canal Zone. He was able to supply silver and gold at very low prices; nobody could undersell him.

I made a great deal of money with Machtinger: actually, a fortune. And I could have made a great deal more. I passed up the chance of a lifetime when I turned down the opportunity he afforded me of buying almost the entire Panamanian output of a certain silver coin known as the "five Balboa" piece. Machtinger offered me that coin, in quantities of thousands, at prices that would have enabled me to triple my investment in a few weeks. But I let this chance pass; I had to. I had lost so much money in commodity trading that I could not raise the vast quantities of cash needed for such a venture.

As 1974 came to a close, I was flying back and forth to Panama on almost a weekly basis. By 1975, however, there was no need to fly anywhere any longer. Gold and silver poured in to me from all over the world—from Machon in Salvador, from Machtinger in Panama, and from the dealers in Guatemala.

* * *

Friedman ended his examination. It was now Benjamin Shedler's turn to cross-examine me. Shedler was intent on proving that my suspicions of Deana having an affair with Mr. Napolitano were groundless and the result of a serious psychological disorder on my part.

Shedler, in a mocking tone, asked me, "What made you suspicious that she was possibly having an affair with someone?"

I answered, "Her lying to me about so many different things, her change in behavior towards me, her not wanting to go out with me, her deliberately befriending people who she knew were unfriendly with me, her telling me things—like my nose is funny-looking."

Deana, in the last few months before she told me of her affair, found my nose just a bit too large and the shape somewhat incorrect. I had to thank Chekhov for this clue. In one of his short stories he wrote of a woman who was falling out of love with her husband—and how, after years of failure to notice, the woman was now observing that her husband's nose no longer pleased her. Chekhov had warned me; his story braced me just a touch. Sadly though, I now found myself examining my nose in double mirrors that afforded me side views; I even began to ask others about my nose. In actuality, my nose was not out of the ordinary.

Shedler questioned me further about my contentions that Deana had committed adultery, asking, "She denied it when you asked her in the morning, is that correct?"

I answered, "That is correct, sir."

Shedler, in a doubting tone, continued, "And she denied it again at night?"

I again answered, "Yes, sir."

And then Shedler with a great scoff asked, "And she finally admitted it the next morning?"

And I answered, "That's correct, sir."

Shedler jeered further, "Now, you want this jury to believe that after these three conversations that she suddenly broke down and confessed and acknowledged to you that she was having an affair?"

I answered, "I would hope that this jury would believe that. Yes, sir."

Deana had given me every sign a woman could give. At first she hid what she now displayed and still I did not see. Everyone knew; only I did not. Perhaps Deana thought I knew. She and Napolitano must have concluded that I was aware; they probably discussed chance comments I made, something I may have said in 1971, 1973, 1975, or 1977. I must have passed them without noticing or spoken to someone who knew of their relationship. Somebody, they had to have reasoned, certainly must have told me. And even after she had confessed and named her lover, I still did not believe it was true.

I added, "I actually didn't believe that even when she said it. I was hoping it wasn't true. I kept asking her, 'Deana, tell me this is all a joke, this is not true.' Because I couldn't believe what had happened."

Negligence Lawyers

Shedler moved to a new subject, asking: "Mr. Yalkowsky, I think you told us yesterday in answer to Mr. Friedman's question that you were primarily a criminal lawyer. Now, as a matter of fact, you did a great deal of negligence work as well, didn't you?" I answered, "Yes."

I remember how I had found my way into the negligence world. I was practicing criminal law when one of my clients had been involved in a minor accident; she asked me to represent her. She had received, however, a very small doctor's bill—$20.00. An insurance adjuster came to my office; he told me that he couldn't settle the case because the doctor's bill was too small. He wanted me to put a "1" in front of the 20 and make it $120. He explained to me that if I would cooperate with him in that manner, he would be able to obtain from his company $600 for my client instead of only $100, an amount too small to be worthwhile to him or to me. He further explained that he always received 10 percent of the settlement as his fee, which was the custom of the trade. It was my introduction to the practice of negligence law.

I asked him to leave the office. He threatened that my case would never be settled unless I followed his instructions. I called his company for months afterward. The case could not be settled. About a year later, I learned that the file could not be found; the insurance company had lost it. I am not trying to say that the adjuster taught me the way or forced me on to that path. No doubt I would have found that same way or path myself. He merely hastened my discovery.

Among the fortunes I made in the many different businesses I pursued, the practice of negligence law allowed me to amass the most money in the quickest manner. That was because the practice was so dishonest—I was well suited for it. But not only the negligence lawyers were dishonest; just about everyone connected with that field was dishonest.

Insurance adjusters routinely insisted upon receiving bribes before they agreed to settle claims on behalf of the insurance companies they represented. Lawyers working for insurance companies conducted themselves as if they had toll booths in the court, extorting money from lawyers opposing them with the full blessing of their employers, who were taking their share as well in the form of untaxed and unreported cash. Insurance companies were periodically incorporating in New York, collecting premiums, and then bankrupting themselves when too many outstanding claims were pending against them. Insurance brokers were doing the same, collecting money from clients, not turning it in, and disappearing as soon as a serious costly claim was brought to them. The greed was uncontrollable. Lawyers were not only exaggerating claims, they were creating a nonexistent clientele and taking all of the money for themselves—unless it turned out that the insurance adjuster was wise enough to suspect the fraud. In such cases the insurance adjuster demanded 20 percent instead of the usual 10 percent. The nonexistent clients we would call "extras." The insurance company adjusters would routinely ask, "Any extras?"

Medical reports were submitted from doctors long since dead, claims of clients losing employment from companies long since gone. The adjusters were not far behind; some were creating their own files, submitting claims from nonexistent clients and pocketing all the money.

Am I exaggerating? Was it that bad? It was worse. Had

not the No-Fault Law passed in 1974, the practice of negligence law would have reached total anarchy. The Bar Associations and the complaint departments of insurance companies were overwhelmed with complaints.

In utter frustration the courts attempted to give lawyers the impression that they were being watched. Every lawyer was required to file a statement with the Judicial Conference of the State of New York telling how, when, and where he met his client. Needless to say, none of us admitted that a cop at the scene or a tow truck driver or an insurance adjuster had recommended us to the client; or that we paid $50 or $100 for our clients, the going rate in those days. We explained to the Judicial Conference that our clients were recommended to us after hearing about our exceptional legal abilities and honesty.

We couldn't give it up; we were making thousands of dollars each week. "Right" and "wrong" were not considered; only "getting caught" was. What we feared most were the token periodic investigations that led to the disbarment of one or two negligence lawyers each year—the only means by which our segment of the legal profession could be cautioned, even minimally.

Somehow I never had a complaint lodged against me during my career as a dishonest negligence lawyer. I was careful never to offend a client. I also apologized quickly and backed away from confrontations with well-connected lawyers from major law firms.

In those days I was convinced that lawyers who operated in downtown offices and appeared on letterheads with numerous names listed along with theirs were men of high moral standing. I thought that if these men ever learned what was going on among us lowly negligence lawyers they would quickly rid the profession of us.

The newly proposed No-Fault Law promised to restrict

the practice of negligence law to benefit only those who were seriously injured. Fear of this law's passing was so great that many lawyers were convinced their livelihood would soon be ended. As a result, committees were frantically formed to battle against the new law. A powerful lobby of lawyers gathered to harass the legislators in Albany. Advertisements appeared in local newspapers depicting the loss and suffering that would result to so many of us by the passing of this cruel law. But the No-Fault Law passed; and the negligence lawyers mourned its passage in 1974 as they would have the death of a parent.

Judges

Not only the lawyers were in mourning. For the first time since I had been practicing in the courts, I detected a nervousness, if not a panic, that I had never before seen among the judges. Rumors spread that there was much trouble ahead for many of them.

The judges' worries seemed to have begun with a story that appeared in *Life* magazine, which exposed Bronx Supreme Court Justice Mitchell Schweitzer for accepting numerous substantial bribes in exchange for his favorable rulings. Schweitzer was a highly regarded judge and a friend of some of the most important political personalities in New York City. Among his closest friends were the DA's of Bronx and New York counties.

The evidence linking Justice Schweitzer with corruption was not small; he had been under investigation by Federal authorities since 1969. It was, however, in mid-1971 that the extent and duration of Judge Mitchell Schweitzer's bribe-taking and criminal conduct was finally revealed to the public.

An accused criminal, Michael Molese, wrote to the newspapers that, after paying $22,000 which was supposed to go to Judge Schweitzer in exchange for a promise of his freedom, he was double-crossed and sent to jail anyway. Molese produced a credible witness who testified to giving part of the bribe money to an assistant district attorney of New York City.

More details about Schweitzer's bribe-taking began to surface. It was learned that Schweitzer had been receiving bribes for at least fifteen years. In mid-1971, at a U.S. Senate hearing, a witness testified that, in exchange for a favorable ruling, he paid Judge Schweitzer $25,000 through his lawyer.

On December 22, 1971, Judge Mitchell Schweitzer retired from the courts. The next day, Bronx District Attorney Burton Roberts said that he was saddened by Schweitzer's resignation. So, too, were Schweitzer's fellow judges, who insisted upon allowing him to receive his pension.

While the New York State courts failed to investigate the allegations of Schweitzer's bribe-taking, grumblings came from other quarters. In December of 1971 Police Commissioner Patrick Murphy proclaimed that the judicial system was "unjust." Commissioner Murphy further charged, "the record will show that judges have been bought, that judges have bought their jobs."

In June of 1972 the New York State Legislative Commission on Crime urged Governor Nelson Rockefeller to act on the corruption that was so observable in the New York City courts. The Knapp Commission, which had just completed a two-year investigation of the police department, made a similar recommendation.

The Schweitzer revelations, as well as the various Commission recommendations, prompted Governor Rockefeller, in September 1972, to appoint a special prosecutor. Maurice Nadjari was the man chosen. Nadjari was asked to focus his attention on corruption in the courts and the purchase of judgeships.

Just as Nadjari was beginning his investigations, however, an incident occurred that indicated what was in store for the Special Prosecutor. The incident, odd and inadequately explained then, today still remains a mystery.

In mid-June of 1973 it was learned that Burton Roberts, who had been appointed a judge in January of 1973, had disqualified himself from a criminal case scheduled to be heard before him, after he had been informed by Manhattan District Attorney Frank Hogan, that someone was about to attempt to influence his decision on that matter.

Right from the start, the case was disturbing. Why did District Attorney Hogan alert Judge Roberts that an attempt was going to be made to influence him when Roberts could very well have been apprehended accepting a bribe? And why did Hogan wait a full month before he notified Nadjari about the episode when New York City district attorneys were required by executive order to inform the Special Prosecutor immediately of any suspected corruption within the criminal justice system?

More disturbing information about that case developed. Hogan equipped Judge Roberts with a recording device to be used by Roberts when he met with the person who was supposed to bribe him; who, as it turned out, did not attempt to bribe him at all. The person Roberts met with was none other than former Judge Mitchell Schweitzer!

Nothing about this episode made sense. Hogan, Schweitzer, and Roberts were the closest of friends. Schweitzer had recommended Roberts for the post of the District Attorney of Bronx County. Roberts had lamented Schweitzer's resignation.

Something unexpected must have happened. The planned bribe-attempt was somehow called to the attention of District Attorney Hogan, who, because it was known to other members of his staff, had to abort the venture before it could be completed. Hogan did not want to risk Roberts accepting a bribe, especially since Roberts was a former member of his staff, and especially when a member of his staff had already been accused of sharing bribe money on another occasion with the same Judge Mitchell Schweitzer.

The additional facts that emerged about this case were all the more disturbing. Seymour Kane, the lawyer charged with arranging to have Schweitzer intervene and exert his influence over Justice Roberts, faced a sentence of no more than ninety days' imprisonment for his role in the matter. According to the ethics of the New York City judiciary, Kane behaved himself admirably. He did not forcefully implicate Judge Burton Roberts. The leniency of Kane's sentence was his reward. The Departmental Disciplinary Committee treated Kane even more kindly, permitting him to continue practicing law, after suspending him for only a short period of time.

Meanwhile, on October 15, 1973, Maurice Nadjari announced that corruption in the judiciary was worse than he had expected. Nadjari noted that he was conducting more than 200 investigations and that several justices were involved in his probe.

Then, two weeks after Nadjari had announced that he was investigating numerous judges, another startling article appeared in the New York newspapers. Judges E. Leo Milonas and Harold Tyler charged that Michael Dontzin, Mayor Lindsay's counsel, had instructed them, when they were judicial nominees, to first meet with Mayor Lindsay's aide, Richard Aurelio, before they could be confirmed officially as judges.

Although Dontzin denied that he had sent Milonas and Tyler to Aurelio in order to collect money from them, Milonas and Tyler thought otherwise. They had the distinct impression that they were being asked to purchase their judicial appointments. The Supreme Court judges of New York City were extremely worried.

I, too, at the time, was worried. I did not know exactly why. But there had to be a reason so many judges and lawyers feared and disliked Nadjari. Perhaps it was because everything seemed to be working well before he arrived. I, too, saw no reason to risk change. I found myself repeating what everyone else was saying: that Nadjari was a killjoy, an upstart; he would bring trouble. I was naive. I had no idea how pervasive and harmful corruption of the courts really was, nor did I realize that someday I would find myself one of its victims.

Maurice Nadjari

During his tenure, the obstacles Nadjari faced were enormous. One of the areas of investigation assigned to him, the question of the buying of judgeships, doomed his work from the start. The vast majority of sitting judges of all the major courts, from the Supreme Court to the Court of Appeals, had purchased their judgeships. During the years 1973-1976, Nadjari indicted ten judges on an assortment of criminal charges. They were:

1. Judge Ross DiLorenzo
2. Judge Dominick Rinaldi
3. Judge Paul Rao Sr.
4. Judge Fred Moritt
5. Judge Joseph Brust
6. Judge Anthony Mercorella
7. Judge Samuel DeFalco
8. Judge Irving Saypol
9. Judge Adolph Orlando
10. Judge Ludwig Glowa

Supreme Court Judge John Murtagh was assigned to hear all of Nadjari's anticorruption cases. Somehow judges under suspicion were often alerted beforehand of the direction of Nadjari's investigations. Nadjari protested bitterly, but to no avail that leaks of his investigations were finding their way to the judges and politicians he was investigating.

The first judge brought to trial by Nadjari was Judge Ross DiLorenzo.

Judge Ross DiLorenzo was indicted in August of 1973. He was charged with having committed perjury when he denied having urged a government official to be less than diligent in the performance of his duties as they related to a certain organized crime figure. DiLorenzo, in his defense, relied on the many powerful and influential judges and politicians who testified in his behalf. Among Judge DiLorenzo's witnesses was a former mayor and several high-ranking judges.

With so many dignified witnesses appearing on the judge's behalf, and the observable hostility that was shown towards the Special Prosecutor by Judge Murtagh, the jurors had to question their own judgment if it differed from such renowned dignitaries. Still the jury acquitted Judge DiLorenzo of only two of the eight counts of the indictment, which they felt compelled to report promptly to Judge Murtagh. The jurors, however, were prepared to continue their deliberation on the remaining six counts, where Judge DiLorenzo'a acquittal was not so assured.

Judge Murtagh was too experienced to take that chance. He quickly discharged the jury, much to their shock, and left the six counts of perjury remaining undecided. Those charges would be dismissed two years later when conditions were more favorable to Judge DiLorenzo.

Judge Dominick Rinaldi was indicted in November of 1973. He was charged with perjury and obstruction of government administration. Judge Rinaldi had been giving narcotic violators and other individuals convicted of serious crimes their freedom when by law the guilty offenders should have received mandatory jail terms.

The trial of Judge Rinaldi took place in early August of 1974. Judge Murtagh was the presiding judge. Murtagh, from the start, displayed his open hostility toward the Special Prosecutor in such a way that it would have been impossible for the jurors to not recognize Murtagh's desire that they acquit Judge Rinaldi. In addition, the jurors had before them a courtroom audience filled with judges who felt the same way as Judge Murtagh and were letting the jurors know this. The same methods used in DiLorenzo's trial were used in Rinaldi's trial.

At the trial's conclusion, Judge Murtagh, relying on long years of experience that taught him that jurors in almost all cases respected the wishes of the judge, then addressed the jurors for two hours. Still, when the jurors took their first vote, six of them voted to convict Judge Rinaldi, three to acquit, while three were undecided. Judge Murtagh, in the end, prevailed. Judge Rinaldi was acquitted.

Judge Rinaldi could not have lost under any circumstances. Judge Murtagh later announced that he would have dismissed the case against Judge Rinaldi, no matter what the jury decided.

These were the conditions that confronted Maurice Nadjari from the very first day he tried to perform his duties as Special Prosecutor.

Judge Paul Rao, Sr. was indicted in May of 1974. He was represented by Roy Cohn, the former prosecutor of Communists.

Judge Rao was charged with perjury in connection with his testimony concerning his involvement with his son in a bribery scheme to help an armed robber who, unbeknownst to the judge, was actually an undercover agent using the fictious name Stephen Vitale. Judge Rao recommended that his son Paul Rao, Jr., who was an attorney, be retained as the lawyer for Vitale. The son, Paul Rao Jr. promised that he would be able to get a judge to reduce Vitale's bail. Judge Ross DiLorenzo, it turned out, was the judge who reduced the bail from $10,000 to $1,000. The scheme further called for Judge DiLorenzo to bribe a Supreme Court justice in the robbery case. The conversations between the undercover agent, Judge Rao, and his son were tape-recorded.

In October of 1975 Judge Murtagh, dismissed the charges brought against Judge Rao, claiming that they were unfairly presented to the grand jury.

* * *

Judge John Murtagh was not the only antagonist Nadjari faced. The controlling politicians and judges of New York State were also vehemently opposed to him. They were not yet prepared, however, to denounce him openly. Governor Hugh Carey was still careful, publicly praising Nadjari on December 15, 1975, for his work in uprooting corruption. Then, a week later, on December 23, Governor Carey precipitously and stunningly fired Nadjari. Until then there was no indication that the governor intended to fire the Special Prosecutor.

Maurice Nadjari offered a suggestion as to why he had been dismissed. Tracing chronologically the events leading to his dismissal, Nadjari related that, five days before his dismissal, the governor had learned that his closest friend, Patrick Cunningham, one of the most powerful politicians in the state, was being investigated for selling judgeships, and that Judges Irving Saypol and Samuel DeFalco, two of the most important judges in New York State, were also being investigated on corruption-related charges. Nadjari suggested that Governor Carey fired him because his inquiry into corruption promised to expose judges and politicians so close to Carey that the Governor himself would not be above suspicion. Carey vehemently denied that he fired Nadjari for any reason other then Nadjari's failure to effectively perform his duties as Special Prosecutor.

Nadjari refused to leave. Nadjari had a basis for refusing to obey Carey's order. He had been appointed by former Governor Nelson Rockefeller, a Republican; only the Republican Attorney General of the State of New York, Louis Lefkowitz, could fire him. Lefkowitz permitted Nadjari six more months to complete his work.

The Dondi Case

The Appellate Division and the Court of Appeals finally solved the problems of Governor Carey and the multitude of worried judges of New York state. In June of 1976 the Court of Appeals determined, in a case before them—the Dondi case—that Nadjari's jurisdiction was limited only to the criminal justice system.

The facts surrounding the case of Philip Dondi, *52 A.D..2d 571*, were simple enough. Dondi, an attorney, was accused of attempting to bribe a police officer to induce the officer to change his testimony as to how an accident had occurred. The police officer, after at first refusing the bribe offer, reported the incident to the Special Prosecutor, who then instructed him to meet with Dondi and feign acceptance of the bribe money, which he did.

Dondi's attorney argued that if a police officer did not accept a bribe and "was merely feigning his willingness to be corrupted," there could be no "corrupt act." Nadjari argued in reply that if a police officer is honest and reports someone who attempted to involve him in a crime, that could not possibly be a reason to immunize the perpetrator of the crime.

The Appellate Division judges were unimpressed with Nadjari's arguments. They agreed with Dondi's lawyer that no crime had been committed. When the Dondi matter was brought by Nadjari to the Court of Appeals that court substantially agreed with the Appellate Division.

The Court of Appeals, however, could not go quite as far as the Appellate Division did in claiming that no crime had been committed by Dondi when he paid the police officer to change his report, just because the police officer had no intention of taking the money. Nonetheless, the Court of Appeals still reasoned that the bribery of the police officer was outside Nadjari's jurisdiction, since it was a civil and not a criminal matter. They ruled, as the Appellate Division had ruled, that the matter belonged to the Queens County District Attorney.

Philip Dondi was never prosecuted by the Queens District Attorney's office. The courts granted Dondi a form of immunity from prosecution as an expression of their gratitude for his services in allowing himself to be the test case that enabled several judges to have their indictments and convictions overturned, dozens of other judges to avoid prosecution, and scores of still other judges from being exposed for having purchased their judgeships. In repayment, not only was Philip Dondi saved from prosecution, he was permitted to continue practicing law.

The results of the Court of Appeals decision in the Dondi case were remarkable and almost instantaneous. Though it received little publicity, the matter of Philip Dondi was the most important case the Appellate Division and the Court of Appeals ever decided. Not only did it divest Nadjari of his powers, it made it almost impossible for successor prosecutors, special or otherwise, to investigate or prosecute judges.

The *New York Times* and the *Village Voice*, knowing that Nadjari was finished, mounted attacks upon him. He was called ineffectual, overzealous, vindictive. He was charged with leaking stories to the press and using unfair tactics in his prosecutions.

The *Village Voice* had already changed its style of reporting Nadjari's investigations of judges after Judge Dominick Rinaldi sued them for libel.

Realizing that Rinaldi's suit could only be determined before judges of this state, and that appeals could only be heard by higher judges of this state, and that large libel awards could ultimately drive them out of business, the *Village Voice* as well as the *New York Times* thought it best to de-escalate their previously sharp criticism of Manhattan Supreme Court judges.

The judiciary's power to counterattack, using the enormous strength they possessed of being able to financially destroy anyone who challenged their authority, was also used against Nadjari throughout his tenure. He and his assistants were sued for millions of dollars by several judges and politicians. Nadjari and those who followed his policies were warned that if they continued to perform their duties, they could be haunted for the rest of their lives with financial judgments against them that they would never be able to satisfy.

Judge Leonard Sandler replaced Justice John Murtagh after his death in January of 1976. Sandler was well chosen by Governor Carey. He was deeply indebted to Carey for giving him so important a position when he had only been appointed a judge a few months before. Helping Judge Sandler were judges Leon Polsky and Howard Jones. Sandler, following Murtagh's policies, dismissed the perjury charges Nadjari had reinstated against Judge Rao. Judge Sandler ruled that excellent tape-recorded conversations that implicated Judge Rao were not valid nor usable by the prosecution, since they had not been "sealed" and thus were not inaccessible to tampering. Consequently Judge Rao succeeded in avoiding prosecution, though firsthand testimony of two undercover agents existed that could easily have convicted Judge Rao even without the tape recordings.

Judge Fred Moritt was indicted in April of 1974 on charges of conspiracy, perjury, and grand larceny for having pretended that his friend Theodore Mann was his law secretary, so that Mann's salary could be used to invest in Judge Moritt's play, *The Love Lottery*, while Mann was living in Florida and not working for Judge Moritt.

Moritt was a direct beneficiary of the Court of Appeals decision in the Dondi case, which permitted him to successfully defraud the city of $26,000. The Appellate Division, relying on the Dondi decision ruled that Nadjari could not prosecute Moritt since the charges against him did not arise in the criminal justice system.

Judge Joseph Brust, who had been indicted in February of 1976, had the charges that were brought against him dismissed in December 1976. Judge Brust was accused of having decided a case in behalf of his former law secretary in exchange for the law secretary's agreement to intercede with the city pension authorities to increase Judge Brust's retirement income. The charges against Brust were based on his perjurious statements concerning his dealings with the former law secretary. Judge Sandler merely criticized Judge Brust for failing to disqualify himself, calling his actions an "inexcusable breach of Judicial Ethics," but did not think criminal charges were warranted.

Judge Anthony Mercorella was indicted in May of 1976 on charges relating to his purchase of a judgeship from Patrick Cunningham, who was indicted with him.

Judge Sandler, faced with overwhelming evidence gathered by Nadjari of the sale of judgeships, held that it was not a crime for a political organization to request payment from a candidate if the money were used for the candidate's campaign expenses.

The *New York Times*, though it no longer held Nadjari in favor, felt obliged to comment editorially that the implications of Judge Sandler's decision meant that nominations for judgeships went to the highest bidder. Actually, the implications of Sandler's decision were far more serious. To protect Patrick Cunningham and judges who had purchased their judgeships from him, Sandler ruled that the sale of judgeships was legal.

Judge Samuel DeFalco was indicted on May 13, 1976, for having helped steer a matter to fellow Judge Irving Saypol's son Roger, which, without judicial influence, would not have been referred to Saypol's son.

The Appellate Division, relying on the Dondi case, dismissed all charges brought against Surrogate DeFalco, saying that Special Prosecutor Nadjari's indictment was defective since Nadjari was supposed to prosecute only matters arising out of criminal courts. The Surrogates Court, they ruled, was outside of Nadjari's jurisdiction. They said that only District Attorney Morgenthau could prosecute Surrogate DeFalco.

Judge Irving Saypol was also indicted on May 13, 1976, and, along with Surrogate DeFalco, charged with perjury in connection with having used his judicial position improperly. It was charged that Saypol and DeFalco met with the Public Administrator, Mr. Thomas Fitzgerald, so that arrangements could be made to have Saypol's son Roger appointed to a lucrative position he was not entitled to. During the meeting, which was tape-recorded, "the participants discussed the use of fictious names so that they could conceal the fact" that Roger Saypol was both the appraiser and seller of the property involved, a position that was indisputably unethical. Roger Saypol, as a result, earned some $20,000 in commissions. Judge Saypol, in return, promised to pick lawyers chosen by Fitzgerald in the future as a form of repayment.

Irving Saypol, like Roy Cohn, was a former prosecutor

of Communists and outspoken critic of Nadjari. During his tenure as a Federal prosecutor, to advance his career, Saypol had no difficulty convicting the innocent or aiding the guilty to avoid prosecution. Altering documents and extorting false testimony from frightened witnesses was his standard practice. Together with Roy Cohn, an oft-indicted lawyer with similar propensities, Saypol managed, with the help of a third member of their alliance, Judge Irving Kaufman, to convict and execute Julius and Ethel Rosenberg and ruin the lives of scores of innocent men and women.

The courts held that, like the DeFalco matter, only District Attorney Morgenthau would be permitted to prosecute Saypol, since the crimes charged did not arise out of the criminal justice system.

The position District Attorney Morgenthau took concerning his investigation and prosecution of Judge Irving Saypol was even more astounding. Morgenthau actively denigrated Nadjari's efforts to prosecute Saypol, arguing that Nadjari had taken tape-recorded conversations out of context and omitted important facts.

Judge Sandler, relying on Morgenthau's recommendations, dismissed the charges brought against Judge Saypol though the evidence against Saypol confirmed his perjury and misconduct.

Judge Adolph Orlando was indicted in February of 1976 and charged with perjury for having sworn that he had not engaged in any "political activity" after his appointment as a judge. Judge Orlando's indictment arose out of a matter which involved his relationship with Mario Biaggi, a United States Representitive who received a $240,000 legal fee based upon his ability to successfully represent a client before Judge Orlando. A substantial portion of the fee—$100,000—would have had to have been returned by Biaggi had he not been victorious before Orlando. In the dispute that later developed between Biaggi and his client over the fairness of the fee, allegations that Judge Orlando was bribed by Biaggi surfaced, resulting in Orlando's eventual indictment.

Judge Leonard Sandler dismissed Nadjari's indictment of Judge Adolph C. Orlando, relying once again on the theory that the charges against Orlando were civil in nature and outside of Nadjari's jurisdiction.

<u>Judge Ludwig Glowa</u> was indicted in January of 1976. Judge Glowa had been charged with accepting a $500 bribe from a lawyer to fix a criminal case involving two men charged with narcotic violations.

The lawyer who bribed Judge Glowa testified before the grand jury that after he offered Glowa $500 to keep his clients out of jail the case was then taken away from the originally assigned judge and brought to Judge Glowa. The lawyer further testified that after his clients were given their freedom he went to Judge Glowa's chambers and gave him $500.

Once Nadjari had been removed as Special Prosecutor, the case was transferred to John Keenan, the new Special Prosecutor. Keenan sought to dismiss the case against Judge Glowa. Keenan's participation in asking to dismiss a case that so overwhelmingly proved a judge's corruption showed how determined everyone beholden to the courts were to make certain Nadjari and his work were denied any semblance of respectability. To accomplish this objective, Keenan was aided by Judge Leon Polsky. Agreeing with Keenan that he should dismiss the indictment against Judge Glowa, Polsky, thought it would be better to castigate the lawyer involved in the bribery rather than the judge. Judge Polsky found no reason to indict Judge Glowa and dismissed the indictment brought against him.

While all Nadjari's indictments were dismissed, there were curious incidental results of his investigations. Coincidentally, during Nadjari's tenure as the Special Prosecutor, Supreme Court Justice Thomas Chimera was killed in an automobile crash, Supreme Court Justice George Nichols was killed in an automobile crash; and a year before Nadjari's investigations began Supreme Court Justice John Galloway was also killed in an automobile crash. There were other accidental deaths and automobile accidents involving Supreme Court judges that were unfairly attributed to Nadjari, because of the supposed stress he placed on judges. Judge James Roe's accidental death was blamed on him. Nadjari's accuser in Roe's case having been no one less than former Governor Hugh Carey. Nobody, however, has ever adequately explained why so many New York City judges died in accidental mishaps, particularly automobile accidents, in the last two decades.

Who Disciplines Judges?

Every case that Nadjari brought against a New York supreme court judge was besmirched, not only by the judges and district attorneys of the various boroughs but also by the Special Prosecutor, John Keenan, who replaced him on June 26, 1976. But in undermining Nadjari, the office of the Special Prosecutor became "confused"; just what was the new Special Prosecutor empowered to do and whom could he prosecute?

A three-way struggle was now underway between the Special Prosecutor's office, the District Attorney's office, and the Judicial Conduct Commission, to determine who would be chosen to have the ultimate power to investigate judges.

In June of 1977 the Judicial Conduct Commission announced that many judges in small towns of the state had been fixing traffic tickets. Gerald Stern, the Administrator of the Judicial Conduct Commission, said the practice was widespread. Stern estimated that hundreds of judges were involved. In February of 1978, the Judicial Conduct Commission announced that 425 of the state's 3,500 local justices were under investigation. It appeared as if a major investigation of judges had begun. In actuality only small-town judges charged with minor acts of misconduct had their reputations ruined so that the Commission could legitimatize itself while at the same time draw attention away from the serious corruption existing in the New York City courts.

While the Judicial Conduct Commission cleverly managed to entrench itself as the mirror and primary agent of the judges of the state's highest courts, John Keenan attempted to determine whether his appointment as Special Prosecutor had any meaning.

Having indicted Judge Andrew Tyler, Keenan succeeded, after a jury trial, in convicting Tyler of first-degree perjury, in a matter that involved charges that Tyler had been consorting in his private life with a criminal appearing before him in court. Keenan received some inkling of what it meant to be the Special Prosecutor when his conviction of Judge Tyler was overruled by the highest courts of New York State.

Still, one dismissed indictment was not enough to convince John Keenan that the office of Special Prosecutor was meaningless; he had indictments of other judges pending. But the Appellate Division judges had no desire to have another Nadjari threatening them. They also dismissed Keenan's indictment of Judge Robert Groh, who was charged with grand larceny and bribe-taking while a deputy borough president. The Appellate Division judges had a very important reason for dismissing Groh's indictment: if the evidence against Groh, who was charged with extorting political contributions, was permitted to surface, it would necessarily have compelled an indictment of Donald Manes, a political leader so favored by the Appellate Division judges that they had to protect him, and anyone connected with him, at all costs.

Keenan by now realized that his job was meaningless, especially after his indictment of Judge Jerome Steinberg was dismissed, despite massive evidence that Steinberg had been using his judicial chambers to make usurious loans, and had committed perjury. John Keenan maintained his title as Special Prosecutor, but decided to become very quiet—a worthwhile decision. It earned him his later nomination to the Federal judiciary.

District Attorney Robert Morgenthau, however, was still not convinced that the Judicial Conduct Commission was in full control of all judicial investigations. Morgenthau thought that, as the District Attorney of New York City, he had some powers remaining that would allow him to investigate and prosecute judges. He tested these powers by trying to investigate an unnamed judge; Morgenthau attempted to obtain from the Judicial Conduct Commission the information in their possession concerning the judge.

Gerald Stern, the Administrator of the Judicial Conduct Commission, refused to give him the information. Morgenthau subpoenaed the records. Gerald Stern still refused to provide the information. The matter was brought to the Court of Appeals. The Commission argued that they had investigated the same incident and found nothing in their records to suggest criminal conduct and for that reason refused to honor the subpoena.

The Court of Appeals decided in the Judicial Conduct Commission's favor, ruling that the Commission and its Administrator, Gerald Stern, would hereafter be the ones to determine under what circumstance information about judges would be forwarded to a district attorney. As a result, the Judicial Conduct Commission was in full control of judicial investigations. Neither the Special Prosecutor nor the District Attorney could investigate judges. Only the Judicial Conduct Commission could do so—and then only when it did exactly what the leading judges of the Court of Appeals and Appellate Divisions instructed them to do.

Every effort that was made to prevent the sale of judgeships and the proliferation of corrupt judges failed. The countless commission recommendations, the appointment of a special prosecutor, the newspaper exposès, all gave way to the overwhelming strength of the judiciary, who still maintained total control of the power to police themselves.

Subin and Kaplan

During the years that I traveled from country to country in search of silver, I referred almost all of my negligence cases of serious injury to Bert Subin; my criminal cases I referred to Sol Kaplan.

Sol was my guarantee of safety while I practiced in the criminal courts. Sol knew just about every judge of importance in Bronx County; his social parties were crowded with judges. They liked him very much. Sol was the wise man of the criminal courts: he was invited to every wedding, he was at every funeral. I was glad to provide him desk space in my office.

When judges called my office, I was genuinely flattered. They seemed annoyed, however, when it was I who answered the phone and not Sol, and would proceed to tell me, "Put Sol on." Always there was a note of urgency when they called him. Observing the respect that the judges had for Sol, I thought to myself that if ever I had a problem Sol would be the lawyer I could turn to for help.

I needed this sort of relationship with a man like Sol Kaplan. He helped me to feel secure in the criminal courts. My good friend Howard Bushin later asked Sol Kaplan to move into his office with, I believe, that same thought.

While Sol protected me in the criminal courts, Bert Subin protected me in the civil courts. Subin was a force among the judges there. His former partner was a judge. Subin dined and congregated with judges; Subin controlled judges. Subin gave me a great deal of security in the civil courts.

Only a few years before I met him, Subin was an ordinary, not overly successful trial lawyer, living in a modest home in Yonkers. But Subin had had the good fortune to meet Howard Bushin. It was Bushin who referred his negligence cases to Subin and gave Subin the opportunity to become the very successful trial lawyer he eventually became. But Bushin did more; he introduced Subin to me. Subin owed his success to Bushin and me; we created him.

Subin would call me every day. We were often in each other's company. We made a fortune together. We were considered friends. He and his family visited my home. My family and I visited his home. We looked alike. We were light-complexioned Jews whose families had come from Central Europe, and who now lived in wealthy Scarsdale. But Subin's home on Reimer Road was far more spacious and luxurious than Bushin's or mine; Subin's home had an enormous circular entranceway, a parked Mercedes, a tennis court, a maid, a wife, and three children.

Subin was a man who had accumulated every material good that man could acquire. Yet in spite of his brawny physique, his charming and dominant personality, Subin's profoundest thoughts revealed that he considered truth primarily a mnemonic device. As he explained, telling the truth was merely easier to do than to lie, since all you had to do was remember what had actually happened. Lying called for altering and conforming your recollections, and that could lead to errors. Subin saw no other reason to tell the truth. His life was guided by a collection of principles of this profundity.

But Subin led me to further introspection. He let me know that just as he could help me with his judges, he could also hurt me with them. Subin expected me to refer all my negligence cases to him and to no one else. Out of pride I refused to admit to myself that by means of subtle blackmail I was under his control. But I did note what happened to Bushin when he stopped referring his cases to Subin; a certain judge who was a friend of Subin began to harass Bushin. Subin had the power to incite judges to harass those who displeased him.

Adultery

Friedman then took over, asking me, "The conversations that Mr. Shedler questioned you about, the two conversations of January 20th—what was the detail?"

I answered, "She said, 'Well, he lusted after me,' that they were playing tennis in the afternoon on a tennis court and he tried to make love to her in the daytime at this abandoned tennis court."

The image of Napolitano, in broad daylight, on a secluded tennis court, surrounded by tall trees and bushes, lusting for my wife in such a spontaneous, romantic expression of love, inflicted deep wounds. Each detail of her romance added more pain, as she described how, in the beginning of their relationship, she panicked when he didn't call her back and ran to him. She was erasing the fond memory I had treasured of her chase for me, her days of deep love for me alone. That love had been transferred to another man.

Deana told me that she didn't care if he made love to others. My wife, my love, was just a concubine to be kept or discarded by Napolitano whenever he wished, and I an insignificant dolt.

Friedman went on again: "Now, those conversations that you told us took place; you say there were hundreds?" I answered, "Hundreds." Friedman questioned, "Were they all in person?" I answered, "Some were by telephone."

Our conversations revealed the ravages of adultery. I called Deana from my office, where I was then living, and in a voice of agony screamed, "You made me even question my fatherhood; you've done that to me. I'll show what you did to me, I have this to live with, the possibility the kids aren't mine, the possibility you married me for citizenship, the possibility that you never really loved me. You disgraced me. You know how I thought about you."

And the way I thought of her: my helpless and darling Deana, so believing and pristine, so vulnerable and lovable, so easily fooled and easily led. Storekeepers would cheat her. People would misuse her kindness. My protection and the protection of the children were ever needed by her: Larin to tell her to not be so hospitable to workmen making repairs in the house lest they misunderstand her generosity; Peree to remind her to take her change after a purchase; Irina, ever at her side and watchful, to guard her mother from harm. I thought to myself of trust funds and a life for her after I was gone that would meet her every need. I loved her so.

I cried bitterly that she could tell me she loved me, when all the while she was in love with another. Indeed, some of her calls with reassurance of her love may well have been made to me while Napolitano was in bed with her, from motels or from his very apartment. And yet, I could feel her love. I still felt a bond. How? I did not understand.

Deana insisted she loved me and her proclamations of love touched me deeply. She really believed and wanted to believe that she could love me again, proclaiming, "I can get that back." It was heartbreaking. She tried desperately, and sincerely, to love me again. She had me make love to her "his" way, hoping that would be the remedy. "This way, behind me"; "Stand on the side of the bed"; "Do something, be an animal." It did not work.

Her efforts to show her love were a painful trip to hell. We were suffering, struggling human beings. We were just two bodies simulating what had once been so natural and that the years had so imperceptively taken from us. She tried so hard, first faking to me, which she could do, but then faking to herself, which she could not. She felt nothing. No love remained and she wanted it back so badly. I could see and feel this awful hurt she had in her.

Deana spoke of love and what it meant to her. She explained, "Love is terminal. Sooner or later one of us, either you or me, will change or our love will change, fade, go away, or die. Yet the real love that we had will never die, it will remain." Deana cried out for this love and what its loss would mean to her. She screamed,

> *Of anything in the world I love you more than anything. That is really love, but I was not allowed to love you. You kept me very distant from you. That's true, Stanley. You don't know what love is. I know what love is—not romantic love, realistic love. You stopped me from loving you, I was there with you all the time. You left me. You've always left me. I've always loved you.*

I could certainly deny my inner thoughts and deny the life I led that I hid so carefully from Deana. I could justify those lies by comforting myself with the assurance that Deana had no knowledge or proof of anything I did. But what clearer proof could there have been than what she felt? Wasn't that better evidence than any document or cosmetic smudge, or hairpin, or love letter? What could be better evidence than the stiff, tense man's body lying beside her? What did she need to tell her of a man who was hers and had belonged to her even before she set eyes upon him? Deana needed no evidence. She knew; she always knew. She knew what I thought, where I went, how I felt; I didn't have to tell her. Nothing could be concealed from her. She was right; I had left her long ago. My romantic love had died years and years before. She had felt the piercing pain long before I did.

Affairs are a leaving. Affairs are love, and every wife knows the moment any husband has left to live that lie.

I did not realize what I was saying when I said to Deana, "If I had affairs I would never feel guilty. If I loved someone, I would feel terrible." I was only expressing what I would have liked to believe true. I was voicing the morality of men of my time—and probably of all time. Deana had a different view. It happened to be the opposite of mine. She would feel guilty if she merely had affairs and guiltless if she loved.

My point of view guided the way I lived my life, as I took my share of romance, doing all in my power to follow my code, which demanded that I never love another woman.

But had I not been free to search and find the women of my affairs, who enabled me to disperse the romantic love that was in me, I could only have done as Deana did, and hope and pray that I would return to her as she hoped and prayed she would return to me.

Separate Families

So many phases, so many acts of finality—there had to be one final statement. But when, and which statement would be the last one? The ending came on June 18, 1978, the very day of Larin's bar mitzvah celebration. That morning I could not find Deana. I testified, "I drove over to Greenlawn Landscaping, and I saw her parked there, and I waited there, and she came out and I looked at her and she looked at me, and that is when I decided that I was going to leave right after that incident."

The next day, after saying goodbye to the children, I moved to Manhattan, first living at a hotel and then finding an apartment on the west side of the city. I then had legal papers drawn up that sued Deana for divorce. As soon as Deana received these papers she instructed Peree that she was not to speak to me again, and that, if she did so, she would no longer be welcome to live at her 8 Dell Road home.

Peree, not taking her mother seriously, made the mistake of phoning me; she was overheard by Deana. For this indiscretion Peree was forcibly ejected from her room, and her clothes and schoolbooks thrown from her second-floor bedroom to the street below. A week later, when she tried to return home, she found her room occupied by a strange man. Peree came to live with me in New York City.

Larin remained in Scarsdale. Although Deana wanted him out of the house, she could not persuade him to leave. However, by the end of November of 1978 Larin, too, had been forcibly ejected from his home and reluctantly obliged to live with me.

Both Peree and Larin confided to me that, years before, Deana had told them that someday they would live with me, while Irina and Risah, the youngest children, would remain with her. Peree and Larin had not mentioned their mother's remark to me, they related, because they did not believe that she had meant what she said.

I could never envisage what was to follow. The suffering I was to endure was unforseeable. Deana refused to allow me to see my two little daughters, Irina and Risah.

In January of 1979, after failing, even with policemen accompanying me, to visit Irina and Risah at their home, I tried to visit them at their Hebrew school. The children were attending a synagogue in White Plains. I drove up on my visitation day, Peree with me. I saw Irina and Risah. They leaped happily into my car. There was no resistance; they were ready to come with me. My car was pulling out of the parking spot, when, from nowhere, Deana appeared, opened the door, and pulled the children from the moving car. She risked their lives in her determination to keep them from me. Deana was not to be disputed; I could not see the children.

A few days later Peree and I tried to visit the children at their home. Just as Peree was about to approach them, Deana hit Peree over the head with her pocketbook; Peree's head shook from the blow. Deana did much more: she stirred up Irina to such a degree that the child, her face contorted in hatred, threw stones at me.

Irina seemed to enjoy what she was doing; no matter where or when I visited her she ran from me. Her momentary glance, just to be sure it was me before she departed, tore my insides. Soon Irina was calling me "Stanley." I was no longer "Daddy." Irina announced that I was never to come to see her unless specifically invited by her. She denied me even the right of expression. She would slam a door or hang up a phone or walk away from me before I could respond to what she had been saying. Irina was pitiless.

Legal papers were coming at me in a steady flow. Deana's lawyer, Benjamin Shedler, charged me with kidnaping Larin and poisoning Peree's mind against her mother. Shedler also denied that I was providing Deana with support payments, though I sent them faithfully. To add to everything else I was undergoing, in May of 1979 a severe sciatic attack left me almost crippled, culminating in major surgery four years later. Mentally and physically I was under siege.

During the following year my separation from my youngest children became complete. Phones were disconnected. We resembled nations at war. I sent photographs of Peree, Larin, and myself to the children, to remind them of our existence.

The process of human psychological defense was at work. If my love for my youngest children continued undiminished and the suffering continued unremitting, I would die. If I were to live, my love had to die—and that love was dying. The children defended themselves in whatever way they could.

Before the final death of my feelings for Irina occurred, I desperately tried to make contact with her and Risah by any means, no matter how unorthodox. Because the moment I phoned, the children, upon hearing my voice, habitually took their receiver off and let it hang so that I could not call back, I purchased a gadget that, when attached to my telephone, amplified sound. I would sit with my ear fixed to this sound-amplification device for hours, just to hear their voices. Whatever I heard I relayed to Peree, telling her such inanities as "Irina just told Risah to change the channel on the television," or "Risah is crying—Irina is teasing her." I did this hour after hour, day after day, listening to Irina playing her piano, water dripping from the faucet, the dog barking, another phone ringing.

More Witnesses

The next witness to be called was my daughter Peree; she was nineteen years old at the time. Peree testified to how she came to know Mr. Napolitano, stating, "Well, when I was a little girl, about eleven or twelve years old, my mom took us to Mr. Napolitano's nursery because he had kittens and he would give us seeds for the garden. After that I saw him quite often on Saturdays when my mom took us to music school. She would drop by and talk to him. And in October of 1977 I came home early from school because I was sick and I walked into the dining room and my mom was having lunch with Mr. Napolitano, and it was really, you know, a nice lunch, you know..."

At this point in Peree's testimony, Judge Walsh jeeringly said to Peree, "That testimony is ridiculous, a nice lunch."

Friedman protested, "I don't think Your Honor should call it ridiculous, that is denigrating what she is saying."

Walsh reacted "Counselor, I have my own remark that I made and I am not retracting it."

Friedman asked, "From January until June of 1978, January 20th in particular, what was your relationship with your mother?" Peree answered, "Well, it changed from day to day. Some days she would apologize to me and say that she was sorry that she was addicted to this man and that she couldn't help herself. And then some days she would say, 'It's all Daddy's fault that I went to see another man.' I couldn't pinpoint how she really felt or what she really wanted."

Friedman continued, "And you went to camp, and when did you come back from camp?"

Peree answered, "I came back from camp in August."

Peree had written to me from camp:

July 5, 1978

Dear Dad,
    I really don't understand what has happened to our family. It depresses me extremely. I keep feeling that something is missing, that something is going to happen. Sometimes, I wish I could sit mom down and really talk to the "real her." I love her so much—because I remember how she used to be. I can't forget that.
    This is a total tragedy! Maybe in the future, the truth will be known and we will be able to understand what has happened—it's such a mystery! I do believe there is a lot more involved in this ordeal than what we think.

    Much love, Your daughter,
    Peree

Shedler then began to question Peree. He asked her, "And didn't she tell you that you couldn't have a boy stay overnight in the house?"

Peree replied, "No."

Shedler insisted, "Didn't you want to share your bedroom with the boy?"

Peree answered, "No, I was fifteen years old. I didn't want to do that."

Shedler wanted the jury to believe that Peree was testifying against her mother because her mother denied her sexual pleasure.

Friedman then called to the witness stand my closest friend, Howard Bushin.

Friedman asked Mr. Bushin, "Do you know Mr. Yalkowsky, the plaintiff in this case?"

Bushin replied, "Yes, I do, I've known him since when I was a teen-ager. I became very friendly with him studying for the bar exam and we both graduated school and I have been friends with him ever since."

Friedman continued, "Will you describe the relationship between you and your wife and Mr. and Mrs. Yalkowsky?"

Bushin answered, "We were close friends, we would visit each other's homes, go to parties together, go to dinner together."

Bushin and I, throughout the many years we were friends, enjoyed long, enthusiastic discussions on all sorts of topics. We loved to talk about politics, our legal practice, court corruption, and, most of all, our being Jews and what it meant to us.

The Jew and his function was our lasting conversation. We discussed our people for nearly two decades: Israel, Zionism; the Jew as a culture, a nationality; biblical characters, anti-Semitism, the converts, the future, and on and on. Deana would quietly listen to us long into the evenings.

Bushin and I were brought up in the same East Bronx neighborhood and we lived our adolescent years only a few streets from each other, and in many ways thought similarly about many issues. Recalling the early 1950s I could remember vividly how fearful we were of the way in which the gentile world viewed us. In those days it appeared as if every Communist that was arrested was a Jew. The gentile world seemed to be convinced that all Jews were Communists. We wanted very much to dispel that slander. We were very distressed by the conduct of our Communist brethren who were circulating petitions to free Julius and Ethel Rosenberg, who we were told were spies who gave our enemy, the Russians, the secrets of the atomic bomb.

We were not the only Jews who felt that way. The prosecutors of the Rosenbergs, Irving Saypol and Roy

Cohn, and the judge, Irving Kaufman, hated Communism as much as any Gentile—and would represent us and show the world once and for all that not all Jews were Communist sympathizers. This is what we were taught and, as distorted as our views were, this is what most of us believed.

Bushin was convinced that the entire world was rotten, money, the true God, everything buyable, and everybody, in his inner core, a fake and a fraud. Indeed, I had to agree that money was truly our religion; its accumulation our proudest observance. We were obsessed with its collection, its preservation, its growth, the interest it paid, and every phase of its meaning. For Bushin and for so many of us, it was the elevator that placed us above our fellow man.

Bushin saw everyone as money-hungry and ready to be bribed—especially judges, who he believed became judges with that object in mind. I argued bitterly with him, defending our judiciary and maintaining that the corruption we had seen existed only in the lower courts; but that there were higher judges with higher morality who would never accept favor or reward to sway them from ruling justly. Bushin was unpersuaded. And when I told him that, if I were a judge, it would be impossible for me to take a bribe, no matter how much I were offered, Bushin did not believe me. My explanation to him that justice was sacred and that the dispensation of justice was really one and the same as the concept of a moral God was scoffed at by him. My further arguments that the subversion of justice was the greatest sin known to man, he dismissed as nonsense. Bushin felt that since I was as greedy as he was for money I was a hypocrite and had no right to advance such lofty thoughts. For my part I thought that everyone had a right to demand and receive justice, and have lofty thoughts—hypocrites as well as criminals.

After Bushin completed his testimony, Paul Osborn, a professional handwriting expert followed him to the witness stand. Friedman asked Mr. Osborn, "Can you tell us, please, your studies and qualifications in this field." Shedler, who knew, as almost any New York trial lawyer did, of Mr. Osborn's reputation in the field, interjected, "We will concede his qualifications, Judge." But Judge Walsh thought otherwise, stating, "I would like to hear a little bit about it."

Why Judge Walsh wanted to hear these qualifications is open to little conjecture. There was no question or doubt in anyone's mind that Deana had signed the checks and documents that she had denied signing. Judge Walsh simply wanted the jury to know how he felt and what he really wanted of them.

Before Friedman began his questioning of Osborn, he addressed Judge Walsh saying, "Your Honor, as I told you this morning, Mr. Yalkowksy, unrelated to this case, hurt his back. He wants to lay down outside. Would you mind if he steps away from the table, at least for this portion of the case?" Judge Walsh replied, "That's all right with me. I'm sure it is not because of lack of interest."

I then left the courtroom to lie down on a bench. My back was hurting me. The driving back and forth to court was taking its toll. While I was outside the courtroom, Friedman continued his examination of Mr. Osborn.

Virtually every document to which Napolitano claimed he had signed Deana Yalkowsky's name to, Paul Osborn established was signed by Deana Yalkowsky and not forged by Napolitano. Over and over, as each document and signature was presented to Mr. Osborn, he would state and restate, "It's my conclusion that the signature was not written by Americo Napolitano but was written by Jhana Sayoc; was written by Deana Yalkowsky." Osborn's testimony was not contradicted.

*　*　*

Throughout the trial there were many meetings called by Friedman to discuss the strategy of the trial. In the meantime, Friedman's bills continued to arrive. The amounts became awesome. I knew that sooner or later it would be impossible to continue. Sometimes I would look at a bill sent to me by Friedman and I would wonder how he charged me $1,200 for a day based on eight hours of work at $150 per hour, when I knew he was representing another client at the same time. I would protest, reminding Friedman he could not possibly have spent eight hours on my case on that particular day, since he was elsewhere. But Friedman would explain that in the evening he thought about my case for several hours and that I shouldn't expect to get his thoughts for free. He also assured me that some nights he thought about my case but didn't even docket the time—hence all that thought I received free of charge.

The bills were so high that when I looked at them I felt nauseous. The strategy meetings, with several of his staff present, were charged to me at a rate of $150 per hour for Mr. Friedman, $50 per hour for Mr. Meltzer, $50 per hour for so-and-so, and $25 per hour for so-and-so. If I questioned these bills, I seemed terribly petty in view of the "free thoughts" I was getting.

Rumors about Friedman's venality and outright dishonesty distressed me. One lawyer at his office confided to me that he and other lawyers of the firm were encouraged to overbill and to add excess hours, receiving a percentage of the billing as an incentive. Other rumors and gossip whispered that Friedman gave important legal research over to other law firms, paying these subcontracted lawyers sums far less than the fees he received from his own overcharged clients, to whom Friedman boasted that it was all his work performed in the wee hours of the night on their behalf.

At one of these strategy meetings, Friedman determined that I needed a very upright and respectable witness to testify on my behalf. I had the man—Steve Green, my former partner and competitor at the criminal courts. Green was perfect. He belonged to the most respected New York clubs, dined in the best-known restaurants, and attended the most important sporting events. He read the best-selling novels, listened to the most popular records, and saw the movies most favorably reviewed by the critics. He almost always said the appropriate. He fitted perfectly into such settings as country clubs, suburban lawns, and dinners for celebrities.

Green was called to the witness stand and, responding to Friedman's question, testified, "Mr. Yalkowsky and I were law associates for about five years between 1962 and 1967 and we shared an office in the Bronx. A couple of years after I left the practice, we maintained a fairly strong relationship and then it dwindled. I would speak to him once or twice a year."

Friedman further questioned, "And in 1978 under what circumstances did you happen to see him?"

Green answered, "I had gotten a call in my office, that he had to see me right away, I was somewhat hesitant. I was sort of busy at the time. He was quite insistent that I come up...well, I went up to his office in the Bronx."

Friedman then asked, "And what, if anything, did you observe about him at that time?"

Green replied, "Well, when I went in, there was nobody working there. The office was dark. All his blinds were closed. He opened it up with a key and he showed me into his office, which was a small office in the back, and it was barren. I mean, there was nobody working there and no work being done. We sat down, and all of a sudden he blurted out what was happening at the time."

Friedman asked, "What did you observe about him as you had the conversation?"

Green answered, "Well, looking at him, it was amazing, he must have lost twenty-five, thirty pounds. He was very drawn. He was pale. He was nervous. I remember him talking and breaking a pencil, I just thought it was unusual, he started to cry, the phone rang maybe three or four different occasions. He wouldn't answer the phone. Either one person, or people, I don't know, came to the door and knocked on the door and he wouldn't answer the door. I said that I would answer it and he said no, that he didn't want to see anybody."

Friedman then asked, "Did you observe anything about his demeanor when he spoke to you?"

Green replied, "Yes, he cried all the time. I remember water was dripping into his office and he brought me upstairs and there was a little cubicle, and there was a mattress in the cubicle, a sleeping bag of a sort, and there was some sort of water that was dripping and he wiped it up."

After Steve Green completed his testimony, my brother Fred was questioned. Fred testified to a conversation he had with Deana, saying, "Well, she asked me if I thought that they could get back together, if Stanley could ever forgive her, I told her that he was very hurt but if she promised she wouldn't do it again, I thought maybe he could live with her." Friedman asked, "What did she say?" Fred answered, "She said that she couldn't make that promise to him."

Doctor Oscar Sayoc, Deana's brother, followed my brother to the witness stand. Both Judge Walsh and Benjamin Shedler wanted the jury to believe that Deana was able to survive only because she was receiving money from her brother, and not Napolitano.

But Friedman then picked up one of the checks that Dr. Sayoc said he gave to Deana and asked him, "And do you see under the endorsement 'A. Napolitano'?"

Dr. Sayoc replied, "No, sir, that is the first time I noticed that."

The check Dr. Sayoc was looking at was signed by Deana and then endorsed by Napolitano. The fact that the money given to Deana by her brother was then given by Deana back to Napolitano prompted Shedler and Walsh to abandon their plan to prove that Deana was financially reliant on her brother and not on Napolitano.

Ada Schein, Deana's closest friend was called as the next witness, at the behest of Benjamin Shedler.

Ada Schein was an Israeli who had come to the United States many years ago. The strong accent of the Middle East, however, still lingered in her speech. Some time before, in 1973 or perhaps earlier, Ada and Deana became friends.

Ada Schein was willing to help Deana in any way she could. Deana employed a maid, Christina. To help prove that Deana was destitute, Schein claimed that Christina was her maid, not Deana's, explaining, "Christina was a lady that I employed who then used to sleep over at Mrs. Yalkowsky's because I didn't have room to let her sleep."

Friedman asked, "And did Christina sleep at the house every night, that is, at the Yalkowsky house?"

Mrs. Schein replied, "Most nights during the week, I think." Friedman then asked "Did she do any cleaning in that house?"

Mrs. Schein replied, "If she wanted to clean, she could clean."

Friedman continued, "Did she stay there and take care of the children sometimes?"

Mrs. Schein answered, "Sometimes she may have been there if the children were there."

Mrs. Schein was testifying that Christina was not Deana's maid, that she merely slept at Deana's house, cleaned Deana's house, and took care of Deana's children.

Friedman was as astonished with Schein's answers as he had been with Deana's and couldn't resist asking further, "Did Christina, so far as you know, take most of her dinner meals at the Yalkowsky home?"

Mrs. Schein replied, "I think she ate there, yes."

Why was Mrs. Schein so willing to lend her support in such a way? And who *was* Mrs. Schein? The closed files of the Federal court provided me with some information: the case of Ilse and Phillip Mandelbaum versus Ada Schein and unnamed others.

I read the case of *Mandelbaum* vs. *Schein*. Froim Mandelbaum, a millionaire who was a relative of Ada Schein, died on March 18, 1974, in Buenos Aires, Argentina. His death had occurred at about the same time Ada and Deana began their deep and lasting friendship.

Froim Mandelbaum had owned substantial assets in the

United States. After he died these assets disappeared. In a Tel Aviv courthouse, a relative of Mandelbaum testified that shares valued at $300,000 to $400,000 were in Ada Schein's hands, as well as other monies of an indeterminate amount. Somehow Schein managed to gain control over assets belonging to Froim Mandelbaum, sold various stocks belonging to him, and, while using another name, disposed of the money through certain banks without leaving a trace.

Unfortunately the Mandelbaums, the true heirs of Froim, did not find out what had happened to the money that was rightfully theirs until several years later. What little they did learn was that Ada had somehow possessed a joint account with her aged and infirm relative that was closed out by her in 1974. How Ada managed to control so much money belonging to a Bolivian resident temporarily living in Buenos Aires, and how she contrived to take the money, was never determined.

The passage of time had hurt the Mandelbaums. Their distance from the United States, their being citizens of a foreign country, and the legal time limits had placed their claim in serious jeopardy. Technicalities would prevail. Judge Haight of the Federal Court ruled that the Mandelbaums were too late, their time to bring suit had run out. Seven years had passed. The theft or conversion happened in 1973 or 1974. The Mandelbaums brought their action against Mrs. Schein in 1981. Judge Haight would not even permit Mrs. Schein to be questioned.

Ada Schein won. Her lawyer was Max Block, Jr.

Max Block, Jr., was the lawyer who, in 1978, spoke to me at his office for an hour or two at most, yet whose presence inexplicably lingered. Block was involved with me and with Ada and with this story. But how? What I did learn about him also came from the Federal Court records: the case of *Natalie Rubin* vs. *Max Block, Jr.*

I learned that Max Block's former law partner, Samuel Kurzman, after suffering a heart attack, had severed his relationship with Block, whom he no longer trusted. Shortly afterward, however, before Kurzman had a chance to dissociate himself entirely from Max Block, he died. Block, capitalizing on the opportunity, hid from Natalie Rubin, Kurzman's sister, the real estate trust that Kurzman had set up for her before he died, which named Block as the trustee. Natalie Rubin was never informed of this trust.

The judge in the Federal court decided, "There is no indication in the record that Block ever received any proceeds. He testified that he never received any proceeds and I believe him." Conveniently, nobody bothered to trace where the money from the trust actually went. The judge, by saying he believed Max Block, solved all of Block's problems.

Max Block, Jr., by the time he began to tutor Ada Schein, was highly experienced in the intricacies of estate manipulation. The Mandelbaum estate would to be handled with greater ease than the Kurzman estate.

What I had seen Max Block, Jr. and other lawyers, with the help of the courts, succeed in doing to the dead and infirm convinced me that when it was my time to leave I would rather not have an estate for the courts to administer.

* * *

While Friedman was completing his questioning of Schein, and I was lying on a bench outside the courtroom, I heard Deana's terrible shrill scream. I rushed into the courtroom, thinking something had happened to her. But it was Shedler who was on the floor, flat on his back; he seemed not to be breathing. Court personnel were clumsily trying to revive him. Richard Friedman pushed them aside and provided Shedler with his own breath; the color gradually returned to Shedler's face. Friedman may have saved his life.

Shedler's collapse, so close to the end of the trial, was heartbreaking. The trial was postponed until March 13, 1981. Then I met, for the first time, Shedler's partners, Allen Kozupsky and Allen Weiss. Weiss asked for a mistrial, claiming that Shedler was too ill to continue.

Walsh responded, "I don't see how I could possibly declare a mistrial."

Weiss then said, "Your Honor, because no one, other than Mark Zafrin on our side, has any inkling as to the testimony and the flavor of this trial, there really is no one other than Mark Zafrin in my office who can fill in at this moment."

Mark Zafrin, Shedler's assistant, had been in the courtroom every day of the trial. Deana agreed, and said, "I will consent to Mr. Zafrin going on with the trial."

The trial resumed and Deana testified. "As a young girl of seventeen, I fell in love with Mr. Yalkowsky. We both were very much in love. About eight months after we moved to Scarsdale, my husband started this business with the commodities, and when I questioned him, 'What in heaven are you doing? You're throwing our money away,' he did what he wanted and, rather than fighting him, I just held everything inwardly and I started to get head-aches. This was in the year 1970."

Deana recalled for me the most disastrous of my many careers, my commodity trading. In 1970, after having bought a seat on the New York Commodity Exchange, I decided to become one of the many men who stood around a circular bar in a large room, engaged in the buying and selling of silver and copper.

I became something of a humorous legend on the New York Commodity Exchange. For the next ten years or so, stories would be told of how brokers and traders would know which way the market was going and what to do, just by watching me, because I was always wrong. If I said "Sell," they would buy. If I said "Buy," they would sell. Brokers approached me to ask what I thought about the market, and then laughed. I laughed too, but it may have been a cry. When you think money is everything and you see it disappear, it is like watching your arms and legs leaving you.

Finally, when I was down to my last few dollars, the head of the Commodity Exchange asked me to leave the exchange voluntarily before it became necessary for them to take away my trading privileges. It was the only way to stop me. In the beginning of 1970, I had had enough money to retire for the rest of my life. By the end of 1970 I was broke, with the need to start my financial life all over again.

Deana was the last witness to testify. The trial was over. All that remained were the summations.

For the first section of the trial, there were two matters before the court: the determination of whether I was entitled to a divorce, and the further determination of whether Deana was entitled to have the 8 Dell Road house returned to her, based upon her claim that she transferred the deed to me only because she was physically forced to do so.

Walsh would permit the jury to decide only on the question of whether I was entitled to a divorce—nothing more. The jury's decision on who owned the house, Walsh announced, would not be binding upon him. He would reserve the right to determine who owned the house no matter what they decided.

For the second section of the trial, which was to follow immediately, Walsh would make the final determination on all the remaining issues, such as custody, support, and counsel fees, which were to be heard by him alone without a jury present.

* * *

Zafrin presented his summation. Pointing to me, he said, "This man is a paranoid schizophrenic...He has not supported his wife or children since the day he walked out of the house."

When Zafrin said this last sentence, Friedman objected, saying, "Judge, I object to that and ask Your Honor to instruct the jury that support is not at issue and that is not the proof before the jury."

Not only was support not the question before the jury, Zafrin was deliberately lying to the jury. I had supported Deana and the children after I had left the house.

Walsh responded to Friedman's objection by pointing to me and saying, "He admitted he did not pay."

Judge Walsh lied to the jury as well. Walsh knew that I had supported Deana. He had seen the checks.

Friedman then presented his summation. He reviewed the evidence of Deana'a financial dealings, stressing the testimony of the bank officials, Amarosa and Solomon, and the handwriting specialist, Osborne. Friedman stated, "Look, ladies and gentlemen, does Betty Jean Solomon have anything to gain in this case? Does Viola Amarosa have anything to gain in this case?"

Friedman completed his summation; it was time for Judge Walsh to present his own comments to the jury. Walsh, who had already lied, tried in every possible way to let the jury know the decision he hoped and expected to receive from them. Walsh had seen, over the years, how jurors would abandon their own beliefs for that of the judges. Not this jury: they had seen enough of Walsh for five weeks. Soon they returned to the courtroom with their verdict. It was rendered on March 17, 1981, at 11:46 A.M.

The jurors decided for me on every issue before them. They held that Deana was cruel and inhuman, and, for that reason, granted me a divorce. They also found that Deana had executed the deed to the house back to me without duress. Walsh shivered; I saw it. His response was that of someone who was as deeply involved in the outcome of the case as I was.

Walsh adjourned the second section of the trial, which was still before him. On the return date, Allen Weiss informed Judge Walsh that Shedler was still disabled. Weiss then cited a law that would delay any procedures for at least thirty days.

Friedman, who had watched the years go by, literally begged Judge Walsh, saying, "We haven't had visitation for two years, that if indeed this matter is postponed for thirty days we would hope Your Honor would mandate that there at least be weekend visitation with those two children."

Walsh responded, "Counselor, as I read the section, I am suspended from doing anything." The case was adjourned again.

In the weeks that followed, misty and shadowy thoughts were formulating. My angry remarks about Judge Walsh and Deana's lawyers did not sit well with Friedman. I wanted to complain to the Departmental Disciplinary Committee and to the District Attorney's office; Friedman strongly urged against it. I wanted to complain to the Judicial Conduct Commission about Judge Walsh; Friedman begged against it. Friedman was becoming more and more worried about me.

Friedman envisioned problems for himself. Judges would blame him for not controlling me. They may, he thought, even suspect he had encouraged my actions. He wanted to sever his connection with me; his practice depended on good relationships with the judiciary—not with me.

Two months later, on the adjourned date Friedman pleaded once again with Judge Walsh, "Your Honor, if we don't resolve the issue of visitation, Mr. Yalkowsky will never see these children." Walsh was unmoved. Friedman made a final plea, saying "All I want you to do judge, is let him say hello to those children."

Walsh replied, "Counsel, I appreciate your emotional appeal. I am not going to grant it."

Walsh would not allow me to see my daughters Irina and Risah, though it had already been established that I was the legal "co-custodian of the children" and entitled to "visitation rights."

On June 16, 1981, Richard Friedman performed his last official act of representation on my behalf. Friedman requested the Appellate Division to disqualify Judge Walsh. He also requested that I immediately be granted visitation with my children, in accordance with the prior orders of the court.

That was all for Friedman. I was on my own now. I represented myself. I had to represent myself. I had no alternative. I had spent over $200,000 in legal fees. I could spend no more. In addition, once it became known that I had filed a complaint with the Judicial Conduct Commission against Judge William Walsh and had sent a complaint to the Departmental Disciplinary Committee against Benjamin Shedler, Allen Weiss, and Allen Kozupsky there was not a lawyer in New York City who would dare to represent me.

Only days after I had sent my letter of complaint to the Departmental Disciplinary Committee, I received a telephone call from Allen Kozupsky, Benjamin Shedler's partner.

The best way I can describe Allen Kozupsky is to present the recorded conversation I had with him after he learned of my complaint to the Bar Association against his law firm.

> _Kozupsky:_ _I don't want to categorize your letter to the Bar Association—your comments are so outrageous. I read that thing very carefully._

> _Yalkowsky:_ _Did you read your affidavit? Have you gone through your affidavits?_

> _Kozupsky:_ _Stanley, may I say this to you, let me say this to you. This is my 21st year of practicing law, and one of the counties that I have more friends than you—when I say friends meaning people that we know as common lawyers and so forth is the Bronx. And when I understood what kind of law suit we had I went to my friends in the Bronx and said, "Who is Stanley Yalkowsky? Why can't_

this matter be solved?" because I always believed that if you can't settle with people,
you know, face to face, with lawyers because
you don't know them, maybe there is someone
out there that knows both sides. But when I
go out and find people talking to me about
Stanley Yalkowsky I get very nervous, because I am hearing about an individual who
is capable of anything, and that makes me
very nervous, except that when I talk to the
guy and see the guy, the guy looks very
rational, very fine to me.

Yalkowsky: All I am saying to you really, is to
read it yourself.

Kozupsky: I have read your affidavits to the Bar
Association. I am saying to you, there is
nothing in this world that's worth the
battle that you have undertaken here. I say
to you, Stanley Yalkowsky, even if you are
right you shouldn't go all the way in this
thing, because there ain't no fight worth
that much, and you are a lawyer and you
should know better. And, of course, going
back to the old expression that a lawyer who
represents himself has a fool for a client,
that goes without saying.

Yalkowsky: I maintain that your law firm has
wrecked my two children.

Kozupsky: Stanley Yalkowsky, you know what
happens when you do that? When you live that
kind of a life, that means that everything
is black and white, but things aren't black
and white. There are shades of gray in every
single thing that you have done in your
whole life, and everything that I have done
in my life, and everything that everybody
around us has done, and some of them have
been good and some of them bad; and you did
good one day and bad the next, and some days
you have been a saint and some days you have
been the fucking devil, and that's the truth

too. And there ain't no right and ain't no
wrong, there is only human beings that want
to live a decent quiet life. I say, with all
the yelling and all the screaming on both
sides, and all the hate, Stanley Yalkowsky,
the matter should be disposed of before
everybody kills each other, because it ain't
worth it. There are four kids out there. It
ain't worth killing the four kids, and no
matter how you look at it, you are doing it
to your children.

Yalkowsky: There is no excuse for what your law
firm did.

Kozupsky: We feel that we are one hundred percent correct, and there is a lot to be said
about Stanley Yalkowsky, that's the way we
look at it. But again, and I say this to
you, think about it, there is gonna come a
time when your kids are gonna be eighteen
and you aren't gonna get them anyway, you
know, and it's not that far away either, you
are only talking about a couple years.

Yalkowsky: I have lost them already.

Kozupsky: Well, I am sorry about that, I don't
like anybody losing their children, especially if you have been right. But that
abomination that you sent to the Bar Association, it's an outrage for a lawyer to ever
make such a complaint. It was so dastardly,
Stanley Yalkowsky, that every lawyer in New
York, when this matter is over, every lawyer
in New York should know about what you did.
Understand at some point in time there ain't
a lawyer in the Bronx that won't know what
Stanley Yalkowsky did here. And what's
worse, I'll expose you, and when I expose
you, Stanley Yalkowsky, you are gonna stand
out there naked in front of the world, with
no friends, with nobody, and your children
looking at you and saying, "Daddy, you are
fulla shit." And if that's what you want,

> *Stanley Yalkowsky, that's what you are gonna get.*

I got much more. Kozupsky did everything he said he would; he was prophetic, his every word came true. Not only did my two youngest daughters despise me, but lawyers and people I had known for years turned their backs on me. Kozupsky's visits to the Bronx were a total success.

I know. I sound bitter and disappointed, and terribly hurt. My journey has not been good. I do not have a good report to make.

It was to be only a few months before Subin, Kaplan, Green, Friedman, and scores of others would all turn their backs on me. I soon would be all alone.

My conversation with Kozupsky ended with a short discussion about Benjamin Shedler. Shedler was not a popular subject. Kozupsky, who knew Shedler was in love with Deana, said "He is enamored by her. He has a personal feeling towards her."

Shedler, a man nearly seventy years of age, was truly in love with Deana; he loved her as much as Napolitano or I ever had. During his years of representing her, he neglected his office and his home.

To express his love, Benjamin Shedler believed that in keeping Irina and Risah from me he would be giving Deana the most treasured gift he could: the gift of her two little girls. This "gift" was Shedler's bouquet of flowers. So, without insight or foresight, and without regard for consequences, Shedler succeeded in convincing two little girls that their father was mentally ill and had abandoned them.

Once Shedler's partners recognized how serious his fixation on Deana was, they decided they could no longer be associated with him. They asked him to leave the firm. By the time they came to that conclusion, however, it was too late; Shedler had already destroyed a father-daughter relationship.

* * *

While awaiting the Appellate Division's decision on Richard Friedman's last request to them, I filed a complaint with the Assistant District Attorney of Westchester County charging Judge William Walsh with criminal misconduct. Within twenty-four hours, District Attorney Jonathan Friedman turned over my complaint, and the confidential evidence I had forwarded to him, directly to Judge William Walsh and let Walsh decide whether there was any substance to my complaint. In his reply to me of June 29, 1981, Friedman wrote:

> *I have received these documents and find no basis for the District Attorney's Office in Westchester County to commence a criminal investigation...I am confident that had Mr. Justice Walsh found any evidence of perjury, subornation of perjury, larceny or other fraud the court would have brought this to the immediate attention of this office.*

Jonathan Friedman gave Judge Walsh the full exposition of my criminal charges against him. There would have to be retaliation. I did not have to wait very long to see what form it would take.

On June 30, 1981, the Appellate Division, Second Department, with Justice Milton Mollen presiding, along with Justices James D. Hopkins, David T. Gibbons, and Moses H. Weinstein, refused to disqualify Judge William Walsh and denied my request that I be given immediate visitation with my two youngest children. Illegally, and without a hearing, they denied my court-ordered and constitutional right to visit my children.

I thought that perhaps the Appellate Division and its presiding justice, Milton Mollen, had made a mistake or that there had been a technical error in my papers, since there existed no conceivable legal basis for them to deprive me of my visitation rights. Another theory I considered was that it had been a "blind-signing," a device whereby the busy justices are presented orders by someone on whom they rely and told simply to sign on the dotted line. I would later learn that my ruminations and speculations were charitable and that it was not a mere "blind-signing," but rather that the Appellate Division judges, led by Judge Milton Mollen, deliberately authenticated Judge William Walsh's illegal decision.

After Walsh received the news that I had made a complaint against him to the District Attorney of Westchester, he reversed that part of the jury's decision which had determined that the house was mine. Walsh declared in his decision that the house on Dell Road now belonged to Deana.

I appealed Walsh's decision. While awaiting the results of my appeal, I requested that the Appellate Division not allow Deana to do anything with the property until the court heard my appeal—a reasonable request, routinely granted by the courts, since, if it were not granted, Deana could simply sell the house, and render my appeal, even if successful, worthless. This request brought me into contact with Irving Selkin, the Clerk of the Court of the Appellate Division, who informed me that my request would be denied. Sure enough, it was. In talking to me, Selkin expressed a peculiar interest in how I managed to afford the high rent I was paying for my apartment. He also commented about the harsh remarks I had expressed about certain judges and lawyers.

There was no reason for my request to be denied. In August 1981 I made the same request once more. It was again denied. Why? I visited the Appellate Division, and again Mr. Selkin appeared. This time he beckoned me to an anteroom and told me that if I left out all reference to fraudulent activities or misconduct of judges, my request would be granted. In September 1981 I followed Selkin's instructions, omitting my charges of judicial misconduct. My request was granted. Selkin returned to me with the signed order, repeating over and over, "I got it for you."

The Appellate Division's decisions were remarkable. The same judges ruled on each of my requests. Appellate Division Judges Guy Mangano, John Cohalan, Jr., Frank O'Connor, and William Thompson had "denied" my first two requests. Finally, when I made the request for the third time, the very same judges granted it.

Apparently, Judges Mangano, Cohalan, O'Connor, and Thompson had never read the first request, nor the second, nor even the third. This accounted for the unanimity. Only Irving Selkin, the trusted clerk of the Appellate Division, had read my requests. He did not like the critical comments I made about lawyers and judges. He showed the judges the dotted line on which they put the "Denied" stamp. When Selkin thought he could do business with me, after I had showed him what he regarded as moderation in my personality (by accepting his advice in leaving out harsh language about lawyers and judges), he showed our eminent jurists the dotted line for the "Granted" stamp.

A court clerk controlled a substantial portion of the decision-making process of an appellate court.

Scarsdale National Bank

Eight Dell Road was the address of my lovely home, located in the section of Scarsdale known as Heathcote. It was one of eight houses on a quiet dead-end street. About a mile from my home was the little town of Heathcote. It had no more than perhaps ten stores, including a branch of the Scarsdale National Bank and Trust Company. Most of the residents did their banking at this Heathcote branch. The Bushins kept accounts there; the Scheins kept accounts there; I had been banking there for some time. Over the years, Deana and I were familiarly greeted by the personnel of the Scarsdale National Bank.

When I began my divorce proceedings, my attorney subpoenaed several banks; among them was the Scarsdale National Bank. That bank's response to the subpoena was innocent enough and certainly official enough. It was signed by a vice-president. Nothing of any importance to me concerning Deana could be found.

But I knew otherwise. A private investigator I had hired informed me that Deana and Napolitano had complex financial interrelationships at the Scarsdale National Bank. The investigator, however, had to discontinue his inquiries because of the suppressive procedures undertaken by that bank, procedures the investigator assured me he had never seen at any other bank in his many years of investigation. The Scarsdale National Bank had sealed all information relating to Deana and Napolitano.

As my first subpoena brought no results, I served a second subpoena on Scarsdale National Bank, dated July 30, 1979. That subpoena was referred by the Scarsdale National Bank and Trust Company to the law firm of Neale, Wilson and Gardella. Henry Neale, Jr., was the lawyer assigned to represent Scarsdale National Bank.

Neale was not simply an impartial, uninvolved, hired lawyer—his father had been the former president of Scarsdale National Bank.

On August 23, 1979, Neale responded to my July 30 subpoena by sending me a letter enclosing certain documents. The documents included two signature cards which revealed that Deana had two other accounts at Scarsdale National Bank, in trust for Irina, that the bank had failed to mention or include when responding to my first subpoena. But even what was sent was incomplete; the reverse sides of both signature cards were missing.

Under normal circumstances I would not have pressed further. A bank, and now its prestigious law firm, had responded to lawful subpoena. Scarsdale National Bank was a billion-dollar bank; it was the wholly owned subsidiary of a multi-billion dollar bank, the Irving Trust Company. I presumed that banks whose directors graced the pages of *Who's Who In America* would never engage in deliberate dishonesty; I also presumed that a law firm whose senior partner was a former president of the State Bar Association would not participate in submitting false documents. But I knew certain other facts. Had I not known these facts I would never have questioned the authority and presumed integrity of such a prominent institution.

I pressed my lawyer, Richard Friedman, to get more information. I called to his attention that Scarsdale National Bank had not sent the signature card of the Greenlawn Landscaping Company account which we had requested. Friedman corresponded further with Neale, and on September 27, 1979, Neale replied:

> *In response to your letter of August 31, 1979, I am sending you the enclosed copies of the signature card which you requested and which*

were apparently not included with my letter of August 23, 1979...

*Fabricated Scarsdale National Bank
signature card*

When I received the Greenlawn Landscaping Company signature card, I did not examine it carefully, but had I looked a little more closely I would have seen that the signature card was dated July 28, 1979. This was odd; the Greenlawn signature card listed Americo Napolitano as the president. But why was it dated July 28, 1979? Greenlawn Landscaping Company did not begin banking at Scarsdale National Bank two days before my July 30, 1979, subpoena had been served; Greenlawn Landscaping Company had been banking there for years.

In the meantime I learned that Deana had other accounts at Scarsdale National Bank that she did not reveal. I thought it strange that I should know so much more than the Scarsdale National Bank and its lawyers about its own customers' accounts. My lawyer, Friedman, also thought it strange that Neale still did not send the missing reverse sides for the two signature cards of the accounts Deana held in our daughter Irina's name.

Friedman, once again, requested the bank signature cards. Neale replied that he could not find them. He claimed they had disappeared, without a trace. No information could be found as to when these accounts were opened, closed, the amounts, nothing. Neale responded to Friedman:

> No information about these accounts is presently available....

While Neale may have been able to arrange to have several of Deana's accounts disappear, and have a signature card of Greenlawn Landscaping Company provided that showed that Deana had no connection with Napolitano's corporation, I had information in my possession that proved otherwise. I had evidence that Deana had signed checks on behalf of the Greenlawn Landscaping Company; I had a check issued by that corporation in the sum of one thousand dollars that was signed by Jhana Sayoc on December 15, 1977.

Not until I complained to the Comptroller of the Currency did Henry Neale, Jr,. finally, after nearly a year and a half had passed, send to my lawyer, Richard Friedman, the legitimate signature card of Greenlawn Landscaping Company. The signature card Neale had originally sent was a falsely concocted document. The legitimate signature card revealed that Deana Yalkowsky, under her maiden name, Jhana Sayoc, was the president of Greenlawn Landscaping Company since August 23, 1977. Scarsdale National Bank and its lawyer, Henry Neale, Jr., deliberately withheld this information for years. Walsh was provided with the true signature card and the Greenlawn Landscaping Company check that Deana had signed.

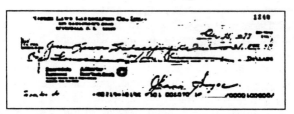

*Legitimate Scarsdale National Bank signature
card, front and back sides combined*

*Greenlawn Landscaping Company check
signed by Deana*

It was strange enough when Neale claimed that the two
accounts Deana had in trust for Irina had disappeared.
It was suspicious enough when Neale would not provide
the signature cards relating to the other accounts Deana
had in her own name at the Scarsdale National Bank. But

when Neale sent my attorney a falsely dated signature card designed only to hide Deana Yalkowsky's presidency of Greenlawn Landscaping Company, I could no longer accept as truthful anything submitted by that eminent banking institution or its lawyer.

In April of 1981 I wrote to John Barry, the vice president of Irving Trust Corporation, the parent holding corporation that owned Scarsdale National Bank. I wrote to him because he was a director of Scarsdale National Bank as well as supervisor of many of its activities about which I was complaining.

I explained to Barry the frauds, the forgeries, the aliases, the nonexistent employees, the missing and false signature cards, and all the unwholesome details of what was going on at Scarsdale National Bank. But there was something more that occurred that I had to tell Barry: my daughter Peree's funds, held at the Scarsdale National Bank, were stolen from her.

Years before, Peree had been injured in an automobile accident and awarded $3,100 in settlement, which was to be deposited in a bank and to remain there until Peree reached eighteen years of age when she could then withdraw the money.

Weeks after Peree turned eighteen, she visited the Scarsdale National Bank; I accompanied her. Peree was no longer an infant and wanted to withdraw her money. We were referred to the Branch Manager, Thomas Kavanaugh. Kavanaugh told Peree that she could not withdraw her money unless she first presented him with a document of authorization from the court.

Months later Peree demanded her money. She would not receive it: the money had already been withdrawn by Deana, only days after Kavanaugh said that Peree could not remove her funds without court approval.

I did not understand how this could be possible. Reviewing the court order itself, it read that Peree's money was to be deposited at the "Eastern Savings Bank." It also read:

> That the said bank shall upon the infants demand therefore, and without further court order, pay over to the infant when she reaches the age of 18 years, all monies held.

How did the money get to Scarsdale National Bank when the money was to be deposited at Eastern Savings Bank? How was Deana able to withdraw the money? Why was Peree told by Kavanaugh to get a court order when the court had said she would not need a further court order?

While I corresponded with John Barry in April and May of 1981, information about this additional act of banking misconduct began to develop.

I learned from the court records that Peree was to receive her money from two insurance companies. I wrote to the two companies. One of them, Liberty Mutual, sent me a copy of the negotiated check they had issued. I was astonished. The name "Eastern" had been erased and "Scarsdale" inserted in its place.

The other insurance company, Allstate Insurance Company, then sent me a copy of the check they had issued. Their check bore more remarkable information: it was made out to the order of Deana Yalkowsky and Stanley Yalkowsky. I had never endorsed that check. Scarsdale National Bank had accepted the money without obtaining my required signature.

While these events were unfolding, I had several recorded conversations with Barry. As a result of my first conversation with him, he consented, though reluctantly, to inquire of other banks to determine if it was possible for bank accounts to disappear. He said:

> *I will ask other banks if they have a problem with accounts disappearing and no records of those accounts, okay? You have piqued my curiosity, that is why I am doing it.*

The next time I spoke to Barry, he told me he felt just as negatively about my charges as he had felt at first, even after hearing about the theft of Peree's money. Concerning the check that was made out to my name, which had been deposited into Scarsdale National Bank without my required signature, Barry explained:

> *In that particular case, if they overlooked an endorsement on a check, then it would be up to the individual who issued the check to them to make a claim against the bank saying the bank improperly cashed the check.*

We then discussed the court's order directing that Peree's money be deposited in Eastern Savings Bank, which instead was deposited in Scarsdale National Bank after Eastern Savings Bank's name had been erased. Barry explained:

> *I would have to go to our lawyer and find out what the ramifications were. I don't even know whether they would take a position in the matter; so if it wasn't one bank, it's at least with another bank, okay? Whether the court felt strongly enough about the fact that it was the Eastern Savings Bank as opposed to the Scarsdale, or Bank of New York, or whoever.*

Concerning my complaints of missing accounts at Scarsdale National Bank, Barry related:

> *That's not uncommon, you know, for account information to disappear. That would be*

*particularly true in an account where there
wasn't that much activity. In other words, if
the microfilm machine wasn't working, then you
would have no record. So that's not an uncommon
occurrence, okay?*

We also discussed Napolitano's sworn admission in
court to forging numerous checks of his account at
Scarsdale National Bank. Barry clarified:

*Now, when you have a forged check, all the
bank has to do is insure that those funds have
been paid to the person that they are supposed
to be paid to, okay?*

As to Napolitano's creation of fictitious signature
cards, using fictitious names, at the Scarsdale National
Bank, Barry explained:

*If an account is opened up under a
fictitious name, all the bank has to do is
satisfy themselves that the person who opened
the account is the person; that's the person
that is authorized to open that account. Which
means that you ask the person who opens for some
identification, or you know the person.*

Barry had to bring the conversation to a close. He
claimed that my complaints were simply matrimonial in
nature and that the bank would not involve itself in a
matrimonial matter.

Barry and the banks he represented were not the least
bit worried about being involved in my matrimonial dispute. They were concerned with where an investigation of
my charges could lead. Disappearing accounts could
explain how illegal political contributions could be
secretly donated. Disappearing accounts could explain
how Ada Schein managed to dispose of the hundreds of
thousands of dollars her relatives could not locate.

Forged checks made out to nonexistent employees could explain massive deductions from incomes and lower taxes for favored customers of the banks. Scarsdale National Bank and Irving Bank Corporation were involved in extensive fraud. They could not afford an investigation.

I might get too far ahead if I tell much more of all that finally transpired with Scarsdale National Bank, events that ultimately took me to the Federal courts and finally to the United States Supreme Court. Very briefly let me outline what did happen.

I tried to hold Scarsdale National Bank in contempt: they had refused to respond to my subpoenas. Walsh, of course, ruled against me and I appealed Walsh's decision. The Appellate Division reversed Judge Walsh, striking hard at Scarsdale National Bank: they ordered contempt hearings and acknowledged full recognition of Scarsdale's and Irving Bank's contemptuous and unnatural conduct. All this sounded very well until the Appellate Division judges realized that the direction of my thrusts was leading into their very own court's chambers.

In the meantime, my complaint to the Judicial Conduct Commission, charging Justice William A. Walsh with misconduct, was disposed of by the Commission's administrator, Gerald Stern. On August 10, 1981, I received a reply from Gerald Stern's assistant, Robert Tembeckjian, the clerk of the Judicial Conduct Commission. The reply succinctly and summarily concluded that, after careful consideration, "There was insufficient indication of misconduct upon which to base an investigation of the judge."

I had complained about a judge who knowingly had made false statements to a jury. I had complained about a judge who instructed and encouraged disobedience of the law. I had complained about a judge who covered up forgeries. The Judicial Conduct Commission found no evidence of judicial misconduct.

Their findings should not have been surprising to me. The Judicial Conduct Commission's predecessor, the Court of the Judiciary, after more than twenty-five years of existence, had recommended the removal of only one judge—and then only after the appointment of a Special Prosecutor had prompted them to overreact to a judge's minor misconduct.

It was during Special Prosecutor Maurice Nadjari's tenure, that the New York State Commission of Investigation noted that the Appellate Division judges of New York City ignored serious allegations of judicial misconduct. It was apparent to the Commission that the New York City judiciary could not police itself.

As a result, in October of 1976 the Judicial Conduct Commission was created. It ostensibly appeared to be a legitimate and independent body, willing and ready to monitor the conduct of judges. To add to its authenticity, its members included lawyers and even laymen; not only judges. In reality, the Judicial Conduct Commission was no different than the Court of the Judiciary; it was still completely controlled by the judges of the appellate courts.

The public and the press were satisfied. Maurice Nadjari, however, was not; he was able to recognize that the Judicial Conduct Commission's creation was not genuine and was designed to diminish the Special Prosecutor's office, and he said so.

The Judicial Conduct Commission, in a pretense of legitimacy, however, occasionally recommended the removal of a Supreme Court judge for misconduct. In May of 1980, at the Judicial Conduct Commission's insistence, Judge James Kane was removed from his judicial duties for practicing nepotism—in having improperly favored his son in the courts. But Judge Kane was from Buffalo—not New York City where the corruption of the courts under the jurisdiction of the First and Second Departments of the Appellate Division was firmly intact. Judges George Postel and Morris Spector of the New York City courts were merely admonished by the Judicial Conduct Commission for the same conduct that resulted in Judge Kane's removal. New York City's powerful Supreme Court Judges Irving Saypol, Samuel DeFalco, and Abraham Gelinoff, who helped their relatives in a far more brazen manner than Judge Kane, were not even admonished by the Judicial Conduct Commission.

The Court of Appeals of the State of New York, sensitive to the distrust that was mounting because of the apparent protection and favoritism they afforded New York City judges, decided to set an example. It occurred in the case of Judge Norman M. Shilling, a minor New York City lower court judge, who was charged with using his influence to try to help an organization concerned with the welfare of animals obtain a permit. The Court of Appeals trampled upon Judge Shilling as if he was the most villainous judge in the state, and voted 6-1 in late 1980 to remove him from his judgeship, and in so doing imposed an even more severe sanction than that which was recommended by the Judicial Conduct Commission, who merely voted to censure him.

Judge Shilling was removed for having claimed that he was a judge with "clout" and "political friends." Shilling, in essence, was removed for identifying himself as a judge too boastfully. The Court of Appeals, by its decision in the case of Norman Shilling, successfully created the false impression that New York City judges were scrutinized as severely as upstate New York judges and could be removed for the most minor acts of misconduct.

* * *

My last hope to avoid trial before Walsh was fading quickly. The District Attorney would not investigate him; the Judicial Conduct Commission would not censure him. I could not get away from him.

Judge Walsh remained in full control. Knowing I had made every effort to have him disqualified, and had failed, and now armed with endorsements by both the Judicial Conduct Commission and the Westchester District Attorney's office, which cleared him of all misconduct, Judge Walsh could not wait to deal directly with me.

During the first week of November, 1981, I requested that the Appellate Division disqualify Judge Walsh. I stressed Walsh's fraud and knowledge of fraud; my request was denied.

Father's Death

That same week my father and mother, as they often did, had driven past 8 Dell Road, hoping to catch a glimpse of Irina and Risah. It was then that my father suffered a stroke. He was rushed to the hospital. He was slipping fast. I longed for the girls to see him before he died.

Peree and I tried calling neighbors. Peree asked one of them, whose daughter was a classmate of Irina, for Irina's unlisted telephone number. The woman said that she didn't have Irina's telephone number and that if she did she wouldn't be authorized to give it. Her voice warned that a call of this kind should not be made to her again.

My father was now dead; at least let Irina and Risah attend the funeral. Not one neighbor was willing to forward that message to my daughters. I begged, but it was useless. Irina and Risah would not attend my father's funeral.

The loss of my wife, the loss of my children—nothing ever struck me like the passing of my father. It left me reeling.

The week that he lay dying was horrible for me. I did not know what a "stroke" was; the word itself did not sound so ominous. His face was clear and had some color; perhaps he was getting better. I did not know his brain was filling with water and that his condition was hopeless.

He could neither talk nor move. One side was totally paralyzed, but he could twitch the other side. My mother, believing that hearing was the last of the senses to go, screamed into his ears that Irina was coming to see him. I stood by him for hours and would not leave. I concentrated on my father. I was able to sense what he wanted to say. I thought he did not like the night nurse; I sent her away immediately.

Before my father died, in front of the eyes of my daughter Peree, he raised a paralyzed arm straight up to me, the one and only time he lifted his arm before he died. He blessed me. I felt him say to me, "Stanley, you must do, and will do, what is right. You are right."

There had always existed in me a dichotomy of spirit. In one sense I was a pragmatic materialist, an accumulator of everything: money, goods, children, women. Another part of me placed honor and integrity above everything. My father's death healed that dichotomy; it was as if my father joined inside of me. There was no division now. I no longer cared for wealth, possessions, or the accumulation of women.

I sat on a low stool and sat *shiva* for my father in the Jewish custom of paying respect to the dead. Three times a day, I read a prayer called the *Kaddish*.

The rabbis explained that by saying Kaddish for my father I honored him, and in honoring my father I was elevating him to a higher sanctuary. I prayed wildly, repetitively, and frantically. I wanted my father to reach the high elevation he deserved.

My father dead; my younger children taken from me; trial before Walsh to occur in days; intense pain in my back. I turned to religion.

The shrieking pain of my father's death drew me to the synagogue. Almost overnight I was transformed into an Orthodox bearded Jew—and would remain so for the next two years.

I learned how to lay *tfillin*, the leather straps Orthodox Jews tie about their arms and forehead. I had the correct *mezuzahs* put everywhere in my apartment where they belonged. I threw out all my old dishes and utensils and replaced them with new. I ate only kosher food. I had my oven especially cleansed and even asked an Orthodox rabbi to visit my home to give his approval. The rabbi was more than satisfied with what he saw.

I would join anyone in prayer whenever I was needed. I honored the Sabbath. I ritually washed my hands before my meals. I visited the sick.

* * *

I asked the Appellate Division, for the last time before the November trial was to begin, to disqualify Judge Walsh. On November 12, 1981, Weiss responded to my request, saying:

> *Mr. Yalkowsky has been diagnosed by Dr. David B. Friedman, a psychiatrist, as having presented the diagnostic criteria found in the condition of paranoia, a serious mental condition.*

Weiss's reference to Dr. Friedman's psychiatric finding that I was paranoid was not merely legal rhetoric. I found this area of much concern. What if Judge Walsh were to declare that I was paranoid? It would sound authentic; a legal document would say, "A judge of the Supreme Court has ruled Stanley Yalkowsky to be insane."

But then, only days before the trial was to resume and while Deana was insisting that my charges that her relationship with Napolitano were a figment of my sick and paranoid imagination, she married Napolitano!

On November 30, 1981, disheveled and worn, I stood again before Judge William Walsh.

My father in his last year

From left to right: me, my father and mother, my brothers Fred and Sam (year 1954)

As I appeared before Judge Walsh

SECOND
TRIAL

Judge William Walsh

Walsh began, "Are both sides ready?"

I replied that I was not, saying, "My father passed away on November 9."

Walsh answered, "I am sorry to hear that but that is some time ago."

I then said, "That is about twenty days ago."

Walsh responded, "All right, well, if you are not ready to proceed, I will dismiss that part of the case and that is where it will have to stop."

Having no alternative, I proceeded to make my opening statement. I promised that I would prove that my relationship with my children had been destroyed by my ex-wife with the actual participation and help of Judge Walsh and her lawyers, who had encouraged her not to permit me to see them.

Kozupsky then made his opening statement, declaring that he would prove that I was a paranoid schizophrenic and that my youngest daughters, Irina and Risah, did not want to see me.

Kozupsky added, "The oldest child, Your Honor, which appeared at the original trial...I would like to examine her under oath."

Walsh agreed, saying, "I see no objection to her testifying further."

I then said, "I would like to question the children as well. I think that would be important."

Kozupsky, who only seconds before had said that he wanted to examine Peree under oath, answered, "I don't think it is proper to have the attorneys examine the children in this kind of proceeding."

Walsh, who also, only seconds before, had announced that he had no objection to Peree testifying stated, "There will not be any testimony taken of the children. You can take an appeal from that if you wish, my ruling now is that they will not be called as live witnesses."

My legal arguments that Peree and Larin had a constitutional right to testify were ignored. Walsh declared that he would interview all four of the children privately in his chambers, without any lawyers present. When I told Walsh that I would not allow my two oldest children to be interviewed by him, he warned me, "Do you want me to send the sheriff to pick them up?"

Rather than risk my children being humiliated, I advised them to appear in Walsh's chambers as he had ordered.

Walsh then began to look for the psychiatric reports that had been submitted to him concerning Deana, the children, and me. Having trouble finding them, he asked, "Does anybody have a copy of them?" Walsh continued to fumble about, muttering, "If they are here, I'll get them."

Kozupsky's Winning Point

The case was adjourned to December 1, 1981, the day the children were to be interviewed by Judge Walsh. That day, in the afternoon, Walsh began the trial proceedings by stating:

> *I've had an opportunity to interview the four children of the marriage, and of course, they're naturally very involved and very interested in what is going on.*
> *I do think that they should have more contact with the father.*
> *They fully realize that the plaintiff here, Stanley Yalkowsky, is their father, and their allegiance, of course is to him.*

Walsh, a kind and grandfatherly expression enveloping his face, then said to me, "These children want to be with you. They want to be with their brother and sister." It sounded beautiful. I could easily have forgiven everybody. Within seconds I found myself liking Walsh. I was ready to extend my hand to him.

It was a new and strange situation. Judge Walsh, who had done so much harm to me, was now viewing me with warm, liquid eyes. Walsh then turned to Allen Weiss and said, "Let me find out what the other attorney's position is."

Allen Weiss's position was not quite the same.

He responded, "Your Honor, the same mental process that he had in charging all of us with being criminals is the same mind that decided that he isn't going to support his children."

Weiss, worried by Walsh's softening position, pressed forward even more determinedly, saying, "These children were raggedy, had no clothes, they were utterly destitute, living on the bounties of people."

Walsh snapped back at Weiss, challenging, "Wait a second, you're losing track of something. Your client is a half-interested owner in a lot of this business, her testimony of not knowing what was going on with Napolitano and denying signatures and denying meeting different people. It was absolutely incredible."

Weiss, refusing to retreat, persisted, "How do we deal with two little girls, eleven and twelve, who know they have been living from hand to mouth?"

But Walsh was not reacting as Weiss wished. Walsh answered Weiss, "If somebody is instilling that idea in them, that is not their father. I don't think they have suffered any such condition."

At that point Kozupsky cried out, "Your Honor, may I be heard for one moment?"

Walsh replied, "All right, go ahead."

What Kozupsky would say would be the winning point. It had nothing to do with what Walsh was discussing; it had everything to do with the outcome of the case. Kozupsky said, "Your Honor, his oldest daughter, whom you met this morning, told Deana Yalkowsky, our client, that her father believes we bribed you in the original trial." Kozupsky, seeing that what he had said pierced Walsh deeply, continued, "What he said about Your Honor is beyond belief."

From that moment the posture of Judge Walsh and the tone of the trial changed drastically.

Walsh decided to take an early recess, saying, "I'll break now and pick up at 1:00."

Denials

After returning from lunch, Walsh said to me, "Do you intend to call any further witnesses, Mr. Yalkowsky?"

I answered, "I call the defendant, Mrs. Yalkowsky."

The court clerk asked, "May I please have your name and address." Deana replied, "Deana Napolitano, 8 Dell Road, Scarsdale, New York."

I asked Deana if she recalled the incident in November of 1978 where she drove off with the children on my visitation day. Kozupsky did not want to hear Deana's answer. Neither did Walsh, who said to me, "You aren't going to prove it from her. She already denied all these things. She's not going to admit them." Deana denied nothing. Walsh was frightened; something about Deana made him worry more about her testimony than he worried about mine.

When I tried to question Deana about a telephone conversation I had had with her and Irina, to show how she influenced the children to disrespect me, Walsh would not allow her to answer my questions. I protested, but to no avail. Walsh responded, "If I make a ruling and you take an exception, an appellate court can overrule me if they wish."

Walsh was talking about one appellate court: the Appellate Division, Second Department, at 45 Monroe Place in Brooklyn, the court where Milton Mollen was Presiding Justice and Irving Selkin, Clerk.

Walsh then said to me, "I told you if you want to testify then testify but don't try to prove it by this witness."

Walsh again and again tried to get denials from Deana by saying loudly to me what he hoped she would realize was his message to her. He repeated, "Let's not waste our time asking her to make denials."

I asked Deana, "Is it a fact that you never made any application to stop visitation?"

Walsh answered for Deana, saying "What difference does it make?" Walsh did not want the question answered; he said to me, "Mr. Yalkowsky, I am not going to give you an indefinite time to flounder around like this. We have to get to the issues."

In fact, we were at the heart of the issue. I had a court-ordered right to visitation; no application to stop my right to visitation was ever made. Deana and her lawyers were required to make that application before visitation could be withheld. They never had. Walsh had permitted and encouraged an illegal act.

I replied, "Your Honor, I am right on point on all the issues."

Walsh was determined not to allow Deana to answer that question. He said to me, "Mr. Yalkowsky, get to something that I can rule on. We are not going to waste any more time."

I then asked Deana if she recalled the time when she led Irina and Risah in an attack, throwing rocks and snowballs at Peree and me. Deana recalled the incident, reciting, "The children started to throw snowballs at you..."

At this point Walsh interjected, "She has been answering every question and denying ninety percent of your remarks."

I questioned Deana further, "Do you recall that you pulled the child out of the car?"

Deana answered, "Yes, there were two children. There was one in the car with you, and going back to the question that you asked me, were they throwing rocks and snowballs, they were angry at you and that's why they started to throw snowballs, yes."

Deana was answering everything and admitting to

everything. She even volunteered to answer what had been omitted. She explained why her eight-year-old and ten year old daughters threw snowballs at their father: it was because they were angry. She admitted to pulling her ten-year-old daughter out of a moving car because she did not want the child to see her father.

I asked Deana, "Incidentally, did you also throw rocks and snowballs at Peree when the two children were throwing rocks and snowballs at me?"

Deana replied, "I hit Peree with my pocketbook."

Walsh could not take any more; he announced, "I'm going to call your attention to the fact that you have ten minutes more with this witness."

My Testimony

It was my turn to testify. This was what Walsh wanted so much—my testimony. Walsh said to me, "I want to know what do you offer to these children?"

I responded, saying, "I offer a home, a father who loves them. I offer a brother and sister who love them as well. I have an apartment that is large enough."

Walsh asked, "Tell us what kind of apartment it is, how many rooms and where the additional children can be quartered?"

I answered Walsh as if this question was meaningful to him and he really cared about my answer. I said, "I have two apartments and they are connected by a door, and in one side I have the availability of converting the living room, I could make it into at least three bedrooms on the one side."

I participated in this questioning, thinking perhaps that this was the way such court proceedings must be conducted. Inwardly, I knew that even if I lived in a tent or in a one-room cellar, it shouldn't matter. Two little girls' lives with their father had been taken from them.

Weiss then said, "May I say, Your Honor, I assume this building is in New York City, and New York City has square footage requirements for the size of bedrooms, and his mere statement that he could convert a room into three rooms..."

Walsh answered Weiss, "You can cross-examine him on that point."

It was heartbreaking. Walsh pulled Deana from the witness stand to have Weiss ask me such questions.

Weiss then asked me, "Now, since 1978, sir, is it fair to say that you have devoted almost all your time to this litigation?"

I answered, "I would say that it would be fair to say that I devoted a substantial amount of time to this litigation. I have done other things as well."

Weiss asked, "Like what?"

I answered, "Well, I read, I write."

Weiss was very interested in whether or not I had "started to write a book about this case?"

I answered, "No."

Weiss, who seemed very concerned with "my book," asked again, "You say you have nothing on draft, in written form, you intend to incorporate into a book?"

At that time I had no serious interest in writing about the case nor about Weiss. I hardly knew Weiss, and yet it seemed that he knew that a book would be written and he wanted to know more about it. Judge Walsh also wanted a specific answer to the question of whether I was presently writing or had written a book. Walsh insisted, "Have you done anything along these lines?"

I answered, "No."

Weiss asked, "Well, is it fair to state that you have been spending fifty hours a week on this case?"

I answered, "In fact, in a way, I spend every hour in spirit on this case."

Weiss's next questions were directed at my definition of the word "perjury."

I protested, "Your Honor, I am going to object and ask what the purpose of these questions are?"

Walsh, who was so hungry for anything that could in some way detract from the truth of my testimony, answered me, saying, "This is cross-examination."

I asked, "As to what?"

Walsh countered, "He has a right to develop his case and I will let him do it. Nobody has to disclose the trial procedure to you."

Weiss asked, "And you also filed complaints to the

Bar Association against my law firm; is that right?"

I replied, "And you in particular, yes."

Weiss then asked, "And you have also filed a complaint against Judge Walsh with the State Commission on the Judiciary; is that correct?"

I answered, "That's correct."

Weiss questioned further. "And at the time you filed the statements you intended to tell the court that the statements were true and you wanted the court to rely upon them, is that correct?"

I answered, "That's correct. We are way off the track now, Your Honor."

Walsh calmly replied, "You have a right of appeal."

Three years later, an incident occurred that reminded me very much of what happened to me when I appeared before Judge William Walsh. The incident, which involved a New York City judge, was reported in the major New York City newspapers. The judge, Louis Grossman, was charged with harassing and threatening a four-year-old boy after being told by the boy's mother that the child told her that his father "could fix the judge."

It was reported that Judge Grossman, after hearing what the child had said,

> called the child a liar more than 200 times, indicated the child might go to jail if he did not tell the truth, and said the handcuffs worn by the court officer were used for people who did not tell the truth. The child cried and repeatedly said he was tired, wanted to leave, or wanted his father, but Grossman continued his questioning.

The Judicial Conduct Commission merely censured Judge Grossman for his actions and refused to suspend him. They found that Judge Grossman was not "motivated by a vindictive or sadistic attitude towards the child."

It was a wonder that Judge Grossman was even censured. John Bower, a member of the Judicial Conduct Commission, voted that Judge Grossman should not have been censured, and that he should have been given only a confidential warning. Five of the eleven members of the State Judicial Conduct Commission agreed with Bower, including Judge Fritz Alexander. They let it be known that they could be depended upon by judges who found themselves charged with corruption. Naturally, there were expectations in return. Bower's extremely lucrative legal practice would certainly not suffer; Fritz Alexander would soon find himself appointed a judge of the New York State Court of Appeals.

Weiss then began to read a portion of a legal document I had submitted to the Appellate Division that contained uncomplimentary statements I had made concerning Judge Walsh's conduct.

I protested to Judge Walsh, saying, "It is so far removed from custody, and it has to do with inflammatory remarks dealing with my claims and complaints against you. I think Your Honor has an obligation to stop it where it is right now."

Walsh ignored me and said to Weiss, "You may proceed, Mr. Weiss."

Weiss continued, "Now, you made that statement?"

I replied, "Yes."

Weiss, with glee, asked, "Is it true today?"

I answered, "Yes," adding, "Your Honor, the purpose in these questions is obviously to intimidate Your Honor, and I don't think you should permit it."

Thus far, on the question of who would be entitled to custody of the children, Weiss had asked me about a possible book I was writing, the size of my apartment, and my complaints to the Bar Association and the Judicial Conduct Commission.

Walsh then said to Weiss, "How long are we going to spend on this point?"

Weiss answered, saying, "If he retracts it, then that is one thing..."

I knew that something enormous was taking place; this was no ordinary trial. I did not want to wait for the trial to end before I ordered the stenographic minutes; I ordered them immediately. I did not wish to take any chances on the transcript disappearing.

While I was in the midst of testifying, Kozupsky began to mutter comments from where he was seated. Judge Walsh responded to these intrusions by cautioning him, "I am not asking you to comment on the testimony." I then said to Judge Walsh, "These children have been told by the attorneys. There have been derogatory and disparaging remarks made." Before I could finish what I was saying, I heard a commotion. Kozupsky was charging toward me. The court attendant tackled him. Kozupsky was flailing his arms and legs as if he were trying to get at me.

Walsh ordered, "Take him outside, Sheriff." Kozupsky was then led from the courtroom.

The stenographic record of the court proceeding stated, "Whereupon a short recess was declared by the court."

Upon the trial's resumption, Weiss asked me what witnesses I would be calling. I replied, "I will be testifying further and I will be calling the psychiatrist. I also intend to call, as I said before, Mr. Shedler, Mr. Weiss, Mr. Napolitano, and the defendant—and the

Scarsdale National Bank." Something about Walsh's facial expression every time I mentioned the Scarsdale National Bank told me that the bank's testimony was troublesome to him in some important way.

I said to Judge Walsh, "There are subpoenas issued on the Scarsdale National Bank."

Walsh responded, "That matter has already been disposed of and they all testified." Scarsdale National Bank never testified.

On December 3, 1981, the next court date, Weiss resumed questioning me, asking, "Mr. Yalkowsky, did there come a time when Mrs. Yalkowsky had Larin under the care of a psychiatrist?" When I was slow to answer, Weiss pressed, "Yes or no?"

I replied, "The answer is no."

Weiss, who probably did believe that Larin went to a legitimate psychologist or psychiatrist, just as I did, before I found out otherwise, asked, "And, sir, isn't it a fact that Mrs. Yalkowsky took Larin to a psychiatrist who said that he needed a lot of help?"

I answered, "The man she took him to was not even a psychologist."

Weiss asked, "Do you know the name of this individual?"

I replied, "Yes, Dr.—Mr.—Wyloge. I'm not certain whether he is a doctor, but he is not a licensed psychiatrist or psychologist."

Walsh interjected, "How do you know he is unlicensed?"

I answered, "I checked that."

Walsh then asked, "When did you check that?"

I replied, "Your Honor, do you question what I am saying is true or not?"

Weiss responded, "I do. When did you check it?"

Walsh demanded, "I want to know."

I answered, "I checked it soon after Larin came to live with me. That man was not a licensed psychiatrist or psychologist."

Weiss, who had intended to disparage Larin for taking a position opposed to his mother, was very concerned with what I had uncovered and so was Walsh. The questions that followed bore that out. Weiss asked again, "When did you learn it? Did you learn it yesterday? Did you learn it a month ago? Did you make this up?"

I replied, "I have answered this question and he is repeating the same questions over and over."

Walsh then said, "We are trying to find out."

There was nothing to find out. What I said was true. Wyloge was neither a psychiatrist nor a psychologist.

Weiss then tried to belittle the effort Larin made to tell Walsh and the court about what had happened to his life and the lives of his sisters. Referring to a letter Larin wrote to Judge Walsh, Weiss asked me if what Larin had written was true. I protested that I could not answer for Larin, since only Larin could know how he felt inside himself. I said, "It's not proper to question me about his state of mind."

Walsh replied, "We want to know what you know about it." Walsh's use of the word "we" was becoming more frequent and his groping for any kind of evidence more desperate as he insisted that questions be answered by me instead of Larin when Larin was ready to testify.

Weiss tried yet another method to disparage Larin as he said to me, "Larin favored musical pursuits and acting pursuits and art, drawing, music, and dance as opposed to sports, isn't that correct, sir?"

I had some inkling of what was coming from the tone of the question, but I still did not believe that Weiss would go that far. I answered, "He used to be interested in drawing and then, say, acting became his most important pursuit but right now I would say music, and then soccer. I really can't say."

Weiss continued, "Let me ask you this, did he have some feminine traits?"

Looking to Walsh, I said, "Objection, Your Honor."

Weiss asked again without bothering to await Walsh's answer to my objection, "Did he have some feminine traits?"

I said to Judge Walsh, "I would like to know the purpose of this question."

Walsh replied, "This is in regard to the question of custody."

Weiss further asked, "Did you ever tell anyone that Larin acted like a faggot?"

I replied, "No, absolutely not."

Walsh permitted Weiss to slander and insult Larin for no reason other than to hurt me personally. The questions Walsh allowed were so cruel and vile that he would later deny that they were ever asked before him.

Weiss proceeded to question me about certain letters I had written to my children. Weiss asked, "Mr. Yalkowsky, can you look at the first Exhibit W-10 and can you please read that to the court?"

I read the letter that was handed to me. It said, "Follow me please and follow my feet. My name is Aniri. I was created by Irina Yalkowsky on February 23, 1979, and I thank Irina for making me. I will tell you more about myself later on. Thank you, Irina, for making me, Aniri."

Weiss with utter scorn, asked, "And you sent that to your daughter?"

I replied, "Yes."

Weiss then questioned me, "And can I ask you whether at the time you wrote it...whether you were under the influence of any drugs or alcohol?"

I replied, "Your Honor, I object to this. I don't think I have to be subjected to humiliation with respect to letters that I have sent to my children that are totally harmless, and to try..."

Walsh interjected, "We are trying to figure them out."

I responded, "It doesn't call for any figuring out, you know it, he knows it. It is like a desperate attempt on your part. In answer to your other question. I was not under any influence of anything and I would write these same type of letters if they were a little younger; I would write that to them right now and I enjoyed telling them these little stories, and incidentally, for you and the court's knowledge, these characters were created by Irina and Risah."

Weiss was attempting to characterize the letters I had written to my daughters as devious, sinister threats. What was heartbreaking was that my daughters were encouraged to believe this.

Weiss, continuing, asked, "Did you keep copies for yourself for future reference?"

I tried again to stop Weiss, saying, "I object to this."

Finally, Judge Walsh relented and said, "I am going to sustain the objection; this is getting ridiculous."

Once again Weiss ignored Judge Walsh's ruling. In the beneath-the-surface conflict between Weiss and Walsh, Weiss prevailed. In this instance Weiss, in essence, told Walsh, *Wake up, Judge. We took his children. We destroyed his family. We need justification. You, Judge, especially. If we can show that Yalkowsky is a threat to his children by these letters, we can say to ourselves, to the Appellate Division judges who supported us, and to the Court of Appeals if it goes further, that even if we illegally took his children from him, it was done with the best of intentions. So, Judge, don't get in my way; it's for your benefit, not only mine. I am going to tie these letters in with a psychiatrist I have found, a Dr. David Friedman, who will later testify that the letters were written by a disturbed person. Don't you see, Judge, we need something!*

Weiss then asked, "Is it fair to state that these letters were prepared by you between February 17, 1979, and March 13, 1979?"

I replied, "That is a fair statement."

Weiss continued, "You never sent them a letter like that afterwards?"

I answered, "Once I saw that the letters were intercepted and used in the same way they are now being used, to humiliate and demean me in the eyes of my children, I stopped sending them."

Weiss began to question me about the psychiatrist I had indicated I would be calling as a witness; he wanted to know if it was Dr. Alan Levy. It was.

Dr. Levy, who had examined me, recommended in his report that if there was continued obstruction of visitation with my children a possible solution would be to give me sole custody of the children. Both Walsh and Weiss had copies of this report. Walsh, however, insisted he could not find Dr. Levy's report.

Walsh's claims that he could not find the psychiatrist's report disturbed me; it was not something that a judge would lose. My instincts warned me to be very careful.

Not being certain that Dr. Levy would be able to appear in court to testify on my behalf, since he may have been engaged elsewhere, I asked Judge Walsh again about the missing psychiatric reports. Once it became clear to Walsh that I might not be able to have Dr. Levy appear in court, he no longer pretended to be looking for the reports. He now said, "I have no medical reports," and announced conclusively, "The records are not going to be taken in place of the doctor's testimony." My instincts were confirmed: I was in an extremely dangerous position. If Dr. Levy did not appear, I would have no medical testimony to confirm my sanity. Weiss would then be able to have his own Dr. Friedman testify that I was of unsound mind, and I would be left defenseless.

Walsh then declared, "We are not going to stand by for Dr. Levy."

Letters to the Children

Weiss determined who should testify and when. Thinking that Walsh had gone too far in stopping my questioning of Deana, Weiss said to Walsh, "I don't want the record to appear that he has been foreclosed of any right. Mrs. Yalkowsky is here if he wants to continue in examining her."

I resumed questioning Deana about the Aniri letters sent to the children. Referring to exhibit W-10, the letter about which Weiss had questioned me, I asked Deana, "Could you explain to us what was frightening? Can you tell me about the letter?"

Deana replied, "There is nothing frightening about that letter."

Weiss and Walsh already had severe cause for alarm. I was establishing that the letters I had written to the children frightened nobody, that there was nothing wrong with the letters, and that their appearance in court was the work of Deana's attorneys, who were doing whatever they could to slander and disparage my fatherhood to justify the harm they had done.

I questioned Deana further about the letters sent to the children. I asked her, "Could you tell me which one upset them?"

Walsh, at that moment, intervened, saying, "Don't get into an argument with her."

I repeated the question.

Walsh interrupted again, saying, "Wait a second, are you asking a question or arguing a point?" There was no argument. Deana was ready to answer my simple and direct question.

I replied, "I am asking her."

Walsh then said, "Ask her a question." I tried again to ask the same direct question. It was as if Walsh had a premonition of Deana's answer. Walsh said, "Who said all of that? Those are your conclusions. That's not a question that's an argument." There had never been an argument; Walsh was desperately trying to stop Deana from answering the question.

I asked Deana, "Could you tell us which letter the children were disturbed by?"

Deana replied, "I don't know. I have to ask the children. They came with so many letters." Then, much to Walsh's discomfort, Deana added, "When the children read these, they said they didn't mean anything."

I continued, "But you do state that at least one of these letters disturbed the children?"

Walsh coaxed, "She said the whole group of them." Deana had not said that at all.

I then addressed Judge Walsh, saying to him, "I showed her exhibit W-10 and she said it didn't disturb the children. I am asking her what letters did disturb the children."

I asked Deana again, "Could you put the ones on the side which were the ones that were disturbing the children." Deana, ever so willing to respond to my question, started to pick out letters to put aside, when Walsh said, "I am going to sustain the objection."

There had been no objection—Walsh was simply afraid of what Deana would choose. He stopped the questioning and prevented me from showing the harmless quality of any letter Deana singled out.

I did not spare Walsh. I said to him, "She was putting them on the side and you stopped her. Your Honor actually stopped her."

I questioned Deana further, "Do you remember what Irina told you was disturbing about these letters?"

Deana answered, "It was curiosity, they were curious."

I asked, "Did Risah tell you anything that was disturbing them about the letters?"

Deana replied, "She didn't specifically say it was disturbing, she opened the letters and she said, 'What's this?' They couldn't even understand your handwriting, they didn't read script then."

Not only did Deana say that the letters did not disturb the children, she said the children couldn't read them. She further explained, "I don't know if the kids knew what you were talking about here because they didn't have any special comment about those letters."

Weiss, who had welcomed this topic so much at its inception, soon said, "The subject has been exhausted."

Doctor Alan Levy

On December 4, 1981, the next official court date, Judge Walsh asked me, "Mr. Yalkowsky, do you have your witness?" Luckily, I could reply, "Yes, Your Honor."

The court clerk said to the witness, "May I please have your name and address for the court." Dr. Levy answered, "Alan M. Levy, 225 West 86th Street, New York, New York 10024." I then asked, "Doctor, can you summarize to the court your experience and your qualifications as a psychiatrist in the State of New York." Dr. Levy replied, "Yes, I'm a graduate of the New York Medical College. I'm certified as a specialist in adult psychiatry and certified as a specialist in child psychiatry. I'm a lecturer in psychiatry at Columbia University College of Physicians and Surgeons. I was the past President of the New York Council on Child Psychiatry. I have published three or four papers in the field of child custody and I'm currently preparing a chapter in a book on child psychiatry."

I asked, "And, Dr. Levy, how many cases dealing with custody matters have you been involved in?" Dr. Levy replied, "Well, I think my first case was something like twelve or fifteen years ago. Since that time, I've probably been involved in more than two hundred cases of varying kinds of problems dealing with child custody or visitation problems."

I asked, "Dr. Levy, did you meet with Mrs. Yalkowsky, Mr. Yalkowsky, and the four children at some time in 1981 or 1980?"

Dr. Levy replied that he did, saying that at the conclusion of these meetings it was his opinion that Deana "had in fact 'brainwashed' those children."

Judge Walsh then asked, "Do you want to explain that expression?"

Dr. Levy proceeded: "This is an event which has been well described in psychiatric literature, in the studies of children of divorce, the one parent is seeking revenge against the now-departed parent, get the children to join in, in harming or hurting the parent. It was very clear to me in my evaluation that this was happening in this case, and I draw that very firm conclusion."

I questioned further, "Now, Dr. Levy, you've had occasion to observe me, the plaintiff. Can you give your observations as to me, as an individual and as a father."

Dr. Levy replied, "Well, you seemed to me to be a reasonable person. You seem to have an interest in your children. You were responding to the dissolution of your marriage with appropriate sadness and anger."

I then said, "I would like to offer Dr. Levy's report in evidence." Weiss objected and Walsh agreed with Weiss.

I tried another way, saying, "Dr. Levy, I read to you the first paragraph..."

Before I could finish the sentence, Walsh said, "I'm telling you right now, you can't read anything from a report. It is not in evidence."

I then asked, "Dr. Levy there are certain items here, all exhibits in evidence, these are letters written..." I was trying to get Dr. Levy's analysis of the Aniri letters that had been so demeaned by Weiss. But Weiss objected before I could complete my question.

Walsh at that point asked Dr. Levy, "Have you had an opportunity, Doctor, to review those exhibits, before this time?"

Dr. Levy answered, "I don't believe I have, Your Honor. I would have to look at them."

Judge Walsh said, "Look at them, I'll give you a

short break and we'll continue with your testimony in a moment."

After the recess, I resumed my questioning of Dr. Levy and asked, "Doctor, you observed all of those exhibits that I just handed to you?"

Dr. Levy replied, "Yes."

I then asked, "Doctor, did you find anything in these letters that were demonstrative of any particular malady or insanity or mental defect in whoever sent these letters?"

Weiss objected and Walsh agreed, "I'll sustain the objection; the doctor has no background as to that."

Walsh's ruling was spectacular. After calling a recess specifically to give Dr. Levy time to review the Aniri letters, Walsh refused to allow Dr. Levy to make any professional comment about them.

Allen Weiss began his cross-examination of Dr. Levy. Weiss, referring to me, asked Dr. Levy, "Did he tell you he was writing a novel about his experiences in this matrimonial?" I found the question objectionable and I expressed my disapproval. Walsh paid no attention to me. Weiss continued, "Well, and if he was writing a novel about his experience in this matrimonial at the time of your evaluation, would that have been a significant factor to you, doctor?"

Dr. Levy replied, "I think so."

Weiss then asked, "And would you have made further inquiry as to the reason that the man would spend his lifetime writing a novel about his experiences?"

Dr. Levy answered, "Oh, sure, I think it would be of clinical interest, because it could be viewed two ways; it could be viewed as his personal therapy, to get out of the depression, or it could be viewed as an uncontrolled obsession with the event."

I would have hoped that Dr. Levy could have found reasons other than the two he found for my writing a book.

Weiss then asked his biggest question, "Now Doctor, if I told you that Stanley Yalkowsky has accused the judge in this case of criminal activity, has accused the attorney in this case of criminal activity, has accused the State Judicial Commission of criminal activity, would that, Doctor, lead you to any conclusion about the mental state of that individual?"

I objected. I was afraid of what Dr. Levy might feel pressed to answer, rather than risk insulting such illustrious and powerful personages. My experiences in the courts had shown me that almost everyone fell before the might of the judiciary, especially those whose livelihoods were so dependent upon their professional work in the courts. I tried to spare Dr. Levy from answering the question.

Walsh, however, insisted, "Let's get the doctor's discussion of it."

Dr. Levy answered in the only way he possibly could. He said, "If these accusations are untrue, of course that is a serious kind of thing."

The trial resumed on December 7, 1981. Weiss questioned Dr. Levy: "Did he ever discuss with you, Doctor, his claim that the attorneys for the defendant received counsel fees?" Dr. Levy replied, "I'm not sure. I don't remember that."

Dr. Levy, who had been brought into the court to testify on a question of custody, was instead being warned by Weiss and Walsh that my complaints could destroy their careers; and that in being my witness, he was aiding me in this objective. There was more than a gentle hint given to Dr. Levy, that he could be remembered when he returned to the courts again. I saw this in Dr. Levy's face. He was worried.

Weiss asked further, "Doctor, having heard thus far Mr. Yalkowsky's accusations against a myriad of people—attorneys, judges, employees of state staffs, state banks, or the Scarsdale National Bank—do you have an opinion based upon reasonable medical certainty as to the mental condition of Stanley Yalkowsky?"

Dr. Levy replied, "There is an old sort of joke, I guess, among psychiatrists which goes like this, that you'd be paranoid too if somebody were following you."

After Weiss completed his examination of Dr. Levy, I proceeded to re-examine the doctor, asking; "Dr. Levy, if you heard that the plaintiff wrote a lot of letters to his children, tried to visit them at their camp, tried to visit them at their school, tried to visit them at their synagogue, called their neighbors, wrote letters to various agencies, in his efforts to obtain his children that were taken away from him, would you consider this a reasonable, appropriate response to what has happened to the plaintiff in this matter?"

Weiss said, "Objection, Your Honor."

Walsh answered, "Let the doctor answer."

And then a voice that had been quiet for some time was heard. It was Kozupsky, who had been allowed back in the courtroom. He cried out, "Let the doctor answer that."

Walsh answered Kozupsky, "I don't need your support on my rulings."

Questions concerning the children and what had happened to them, apparently plagued Kozupsky with guilt; nothing seemed to disturb Weiss.

Dr. Levy gave his answer. "I would say that if a parent was separated from his children, his or her children, and made every attempt to see them, and to go where they go, that sounds like a normal kind of thing in these circumstances."

I was so sick and exhausted at this point that I did not believe I could continue. I asked, "Dr. Levy, you've had a chance to observe me in this court, and this question I'm going to ask relates to my condition at this very moment. Do I appear to you to be very tired and under a great deal of strain?"

Dr. Levy replied, "Yes."

Walsh then said, "The doctor says he looks tired and we all agree to that."

Though I was exhausted, I proceeded as best I could, reminding Judge Walsh that Deana had not completed her financial questionnaire, which was required by the court to be filled out by litigants in matrimonial actions. Deana did not fill in the blank spaces that asked her to "List all assets transferred in any manner during the preceding three years." Walsh had Deana's incomplete financial questionnaire in his hands.

Weiss responded, "She says she does not have any assets and that is the testimony."

Walsh then said, "Thank you. We'll start at 9:30 tomorrow morning." But the next morning, I could not come to court; I could not get out of my bed.

* * *

While I was at home, Allen Weiss called me. We had the following recorded conversation:

> Weiss: Hello, this is Allen Weiss, what's your problem? Let me just tell you, just offhand, you are a very, very shrewd, calculating, sophisticated, experienced businessman. I see by your gold and silver transactions and

by your importing of coins, what have you—you have been around; you are very calculating.

Yalkowsky: No, I am not calculating, I have been around but I am not calculating.

Weiss: I don't know what you want—you want to hurt back? You want to become a legend?

Yalkowsky: I have done nothing other than try to get my children back.

Weiss: Have you done everything on the up and up?

Yalkowsky: I don't know. I have not; not everything.

Weiss: All right. There are a lot of transactions that I see that you have been involved with that I know haven't been on the up and up. You want to be like a good father to your daughters—you act like a father, Mister. No one wants to take your children away from you.

Yalkowsky: They are away from me.

Weiss: It's your attitude that's been a case against you.

Yalkowsky: What kind of attitude? I haven't spoken to them in a couple of years.

Weiss: Why don't you bring your mother and brother in?

Yalkowsky: This has nothing to do with my parents.

Weiss: If you want to carry it on and on and on, you are paying the price; I am not.

Yalkowsky: Well, nobody wants to carry anything

*on and on and on, and I certainly don't want
to carry it on and on and on.*

*Weiss: It's that you are so right and so correct
and your position is so virtuous, and you
would want this court to act quickly so you
can get visitation and yet you just prefer
to continue to jab like this was some kind
of army maneuver, you know, you jab and you
retreat.*

*Yalkowsky: Like I said, Mr. Weiss, I don't want
to be impolite and I certainly don't want to
hang up on you, I really don't.*

*Weiss: Let me just ask you one thing, and I am
speaking to you. I subpoenaed your brother
and your mother. Are they gonna come to
court?*

Weiss was heartlessly cruel. His slanders of my son
and threats to torment my mother while she was in
mourning were relentless.

Doctor David Friedman

On Monday December 14, 1981, Weiss called to the stand his star witness, Dr. David Friedman.

After Dr. Friedman recited his educational background and professional attainments, which were reasonably impressive, Allen Weiss asked him, "Based upon your medical examination of Mr. Yalkowsky on September 21, on September 16, 22, and 24, did you diagnose a mental condition?"

Dr. Friedman responded, "I did."

Weiss questioned, "And can you state what you found Mr. Yalkowsky to have?"

Dr. Friedman replied, "If I can read from my report, it would be much more concise."

Walsh, who had steadfastly refused to permit Dr. Levy to read from his medical report, answered, "Certainly."

Dr. Friedman read, "Mr. Yalkowsky presented the diagnostic criteria of the American Psychiatric Association, the condition of paranoia, which is a serious mental condition."

Weiss then asked, "Now, Doctor, can you tell us what the criteria for a diagnosis of paranoia, a serious mental disorder, is?"

Dr. Friedman answered, "Paranoia involves the following diagnostic criteria. Persistent persecutory delusions; the persecutory delusions came about in two areas. One involving his wife—he said that she was brainwashing the children, and I asked him how he knew that; and he said he just knew it. He, at one point, claimed that I was a friend of the attorney, Mr. Shedler, and he said I had been in direct contact with Mr. Shedler all the time, and I asked him how he knew that, and he said he knew that. When I said to him that his children, the two younger daughters, elected to stay with the mother, when I had seen them, he then became furious with me. He said I will now call you 'mister' and proceeded to call me mister."

Weiss asked, "What significance, if any, was there to his reference to you as 'mister' rather than doctor?"

Dr. Friedman replied, "He may disagree with me, but it is not up to him to decide whether I'm a mister or a doctor; the State of New York has decided that."

Weiss asked, "And is that, in your opinion, an indication of paranoia?"

Dr. Friedman replied, "Yes, and a grandiosity."

Weiss continued, "Now, assuming, Doctor, that at the time Mr. Yalkowsky allegedly learned of his wife's actions, that he stated that 'I fell down, I cried, I rolled on the rug, I bit the rug, I foamed at the mouth; I just completely fell apart, I cried for I'd say, at least 30 straight days'—assuming that he had stated that to you, would that in any way affect your diagnosis of Mr. Yalkowsky's mental condition?"

Dr. Friedman answered, "Well, I would find this most unusual in that if this man felt that his wife had been unfaithful to act in that way would be in my way of thinking inappropriate."

Weiss then handed to Dr. Friedman one of the affidavits I had submitted to the court that was critical of Judge Walsh.

Weiss asked, "Is it helpful in connection with your diagnosis to read and examine reports and statements made by the subject of the investigation?"

Dr. Friedman replied, "Sometimes vital."

Weiss asked again, "Vital?"

Dr. Freidman repeated, "Vital."

Weiss continued, "Doctor, having examined those claims, and based upon your interviews with Mr. Yalkowsky in September of 1980, do you have an opinion as to whether the condition that Mr. Yalkowsky suffered from has increased or abated in any respect?"

Dr. Friedman replied, "I would definitely, in my opinion, say that the condition has worsened or increased, as you put it." Dr. Friedman continued, "When I read this document that you referred to, not only does he make statements which he cannot prove, which seem blatantly untrue, but..."

Judge Walsh at that point interjected, "Just a second, you can't assume they are true or untrue. If he had believed them to be true, you don't know whether they are true or not."

Dr. Friedman replied, "I said 'assumed.' I'm very careful of the words I use."

Judge Walsh answered, "I hope so."

Weiss then asked Dr. Friedman, "These sweeping generalizations that Mr. Yalkowsky makes, do they in any way change or alter your diagnosis of his mental condition which you found in September of 1980?"

Dr. Friedman replied, "I am now entertaining a more serious diagnosis on the basis of this, what I would consider poor judgment, in which he involves the judge in the courtroom, that he is trying his own case, to the possible diagnosis of paranoid schizophrenia which I could not make at the time, at the time I first examined him."

Thinking that it would please Judge Walsh if he promoted my condition to a more serious diagnosis, for my having submitted an affidavit critical of the judge, Dr. Friedman was willing to label me a paranoid schizophrenic, a malady so serious that it usually requires confinement of those afflicted. Judge Walsh, who counted heavily on Dr. Friedman making a respectable presentation, once he heard Dr. Friedman's testimony, was terribly disappointed by the doctor's comments, especially after he heard his reasons for concluding that I was suffering from paranoia.

Weiss asked, "If you found, doctor, that Mr. Yalkowsky didn't provide any support for his wife and children since October of 1979 to date, would that information be of value diagnosing Mr. Yalkowsky's condition?"

Dr. Friedman answered, "Yes."

Weiss continued, "And is that a symptom of the paranoia psychosis?"

Dr. Friedman again answered, "Yes."

Weiss asked, "Doctor, does a person who suffers from the paranoia described, is that person, can that person be dangerous to his own children?"

Dr. Friedman answered, "Yes."

Weiss continued, "And can you tell us what the danger is?"

Dr. Friedman answered, "If he sees the children as part of the persecutors or getting into the camp of the persecutors, he can then take his anger out against the children."

Weiss questioned further, "And can you tell us whether it would be in the best interest of the children, where the parent is suffering from paranoia that is untreated and not under medical treatment, would it be dangerous for those children to visit with their parent in an unsupervised setting?"

Dr. Friedman replied, "I would think so."

Weiss concluded his questioning of Dr. Friedman. It was my turn to cross-examine him.

I asked, "Doctor, would it be fair to say that if many of the facts or a good many of the facts that I said to you were, in fact, true, that would take away the fixed false beliefs premise and the whole system of paranoia would then fall, wouldn't you say that is correct?"

Dr. Friedman answered, "No. I'll tell you. A lot of your behavior seemed quite unusual to me. Your wife allegedly was unfaithful at the time you came to see me; which I say allegedly, I couldn't be the one to determine that. Your behavior in regard to that was most unusual in so far as you stayed there for six months, and you begged, you pleaded, according to what you told me, and I have subsequently learned about your throwing yourself on the floor and so on; your alternation in mood, which was very rapid, even in your telephone conversations with me, all of these fit into my conceptionalization of you having a condition I call paranoia. Again, I have to emphasize one thing, that it is not one thing that made me conclude what I did."

I then asked, "However, so in other words, aside from fixed belief you're now adding something to the definition, saying if somebody cries or tries to stay home with his wife for six months to try to make the marriage stay together, that is also something to consider paranoid, is that correct?"

Dr. Friedman responded, "Mr. Yalkowsky, if you'll forgive me, there is data that you are omitting. For somebody who presumed to be that interested in his children, on the basis of what your children had told me, not what you had told me, they said you hadn't spent that much time with them and if that is not true, then I would have to revise my statement."

I then challenged, "You would have to revise your statement, in fact, even if it were true. Isn't that something else other than paranoia when a father doesn't spend time with the children?"

Dr. Friedman explained, "You're taking this out of context. I'm focusing in on inconsistencies. Your avowed love for your children was not based upon your previous behavior prior to this litigation."

I then questioned, "And would you consider that a factor of paranoia or something else?"

Dr. Friedman modified, "A factor of inconsistency, not paranoia."

I continued, "So when we go back to paranoia, if the fixed system is not false, but true, there is no paranoia. Is that correct?"

Dr. Friedman answered, "That is true."

Although Dr. Friedman could have testified further, Judge Walsh interrupted the questioning, saying, "I think we have the picture pretty clear from this witness. I'll excuse you, Doctor. Thank you very much. It is now five after 1:00." Walsh wanted Dr. Friedman off the witness stand. By now Weiss wanted him off the stand just as much as Walsh. Before Dr. Friedman left the witness stand, however, he asked to make a correction in his testimony. Walsh permitted him to do so. Dr. Friedman then withdrew his diagnosis that I was a paranoid schizophrenic.

Powdered Milk

Weiss then began to make certain statements under the legal theory known as an "offer of proof."

Weiss declared, "I offer to show that Mr. Yalkowsky was a principal of a corporation organized, I believe, in the Philippines, in 1976, called Silkan Enterprises, which corporation was engaged in the sale of milk and that..."

Walsh, not sure he was hearing correctly, interjected, "Did you say milk?"

Weiss replied, "Yes, and that there was another person identified by letter as B.O.Y., who is Benedicto. The correspondence would speak for itself concerning the conduct of this person with Mr. Yalkowsky."

Weiss was referring to what I believe had been my last great adventure. Sometime in 1976 Deana's brother-in-law approached me with this most remarkable proposition. In the years that had passed since Benedicto helped in the release of my seized coins, his close relationship to the inner circle of controlling and influential families of the Philippines advanced his fortunes and position dramatically. He was now able to offer me the position of agent to purchase the entire powdered milk needs of the Philippine Islands, a roughly 100-million-dollars-per-year expenditure, that was traditionally purchased from the New Zealand Dairy Board. The net price was to be $485 per metric ton C.I.F. Manila, with a prospect of four shipments per year of 50,000 metric tons per shipment. The contract was to be in effect for two years. The commission to Silkan Corporation was to be $60 per ton.

Throughout early and middle 1976 I was thoroughly immersed in negotiating a multi-million-dollar international transaction. I opened an account in Panama for the Silkan Enterprises Corporation. Panama, it was decided, was where I would receive my commission and where my Filipino collaborators and I would have reserved and preserved for ourselves enough money to last us the rest of our lives.

What amazed me most about the transaction was its credibility. Over the years I had been approached with propositions, from buying arms for revolutions to digging for buried treasures, but I could usually sense if the proposition was not legitimate. Not with this.

I did extensive research on powdered milk and its market. My discussions were soon quite knowledgeable. As the weeks of negotiating passed into months, I received detailed competitive bids from several nations.

My work had a value. I made arrangements with certain Western European nations that would have enabled the Philippines to obtain quality powdered milk at a substantially lower price than what they had been paying New Zealand throughout their many years of buying milk from that country.

As a result of my negotiations, a major meeting was requested by the New Zealand Dairy Board. They were clamoring for a contract. They were pursuing me. The New Zealand Dairy Board was prepared to lower its price for powdered milk and send the commission fees I had requested to the Silkan Corporation in Panama. All the Dairy Board wanted was confirmation from someone with authority in the Philippines so that they could safely transfer the funds to me. This request was obviously reasonable.

Benedicto asked that I come to the Philippines immediately. Multimillions of dollars were involved, and the conferring of a commission upon me by a suitable person of authority in the Philippines required my immediate attendance.

I decided not to go. Some instinct warned me that if I went to the Philippines, I would either be killed or kidnapped. The venture was over.

Weiss continued with his offers, saying, "I offer to show by exhibits that Mr. Yalkowsky, in 1976, together with the individual referred to as B.O.Y., earlier was engaged in the illicit smuggling of General Yamashita's treasure hidden in several places, which he acquired in the war campaign in Malaya and Singapore."

Walsh asked, "Whose campaign?"

Weiss replied, "General Yamashita."

Walsh facetiously responded, "I didn't know whether Mr. Yalkowsky was involved in the campaign."

I had not the vaguest idea of who or what Weiss was talking about. At the time I had never heard of General Tomoyuki Yamashita. When I later read about him, I learned that he was a remarkably able general who, during World War II, took command of the Japanese forces occupying the Philippines. I would also learn that General Yamashita had been convicted by a United States military tribunal of crimes he did not commit; and executed simply for being a general on the losing side.

Weiss continued, "I would also offer the records and documents I have subpoenaed from an attorney named Burt Subin. He told me over the past four years he paid Mr. Yalkowsky hundreds of thousands of dollars as Mr. Yalkowsky's share of legal fees in negligence matters that Mr. Yalkowsky referred to Mr. Subin."

Subin had told Weiss the truth. Subin had paid me hundreds of thousands of dollars and owed me yet hundreds of thousands more.

Weiss was trying to establish that I was wealthy. I never disputed this claim. I simply did not believe that

Weiss or any of Deana's lawyers were entitled to have their legal fees paid by me based on their claim that Deana was destitute. The case was adjourned to the next day, December 15, 1981.

Deana and Shedler Testify

On the morning of December 15, 1981, Weiss announced, "I will now call Mrs. Yalkowsky." Walsh instructed Deana, "You've already been sworn in this proceeding. You'll continue to testify under oath."

Weiss then asked Deana a perfectly appropriate question; "Mrs. Yalkowsky, do you have any savings account in any bank?"

Walsh, knowing that Deana could very easily start reading off a list of bank accounts, almost jumped out of his seat to stop Deana from answering the question. Walsh interjected, "No, wait a second, any financial statement has to be submitted with her financial statement." Walsh hoped that his incoherent gibberish would prompt Weiss to understand that it was best not to ask Deana such questions.

Weiss, not yet quite comprehending Walsh's direction, responded, "Her financial statement was submitted to Your Honor."

Walsh, exhausted by Weiss's inability to comprehend what he was doing, elaborated further, "Whenever a form is left blank, I've said this several times, it is assumed to be a negative answer." This was Walsh's solution; the only way Walsh could be sure that Deana denied her assets and accounts was to make sure she did not answer any questions relating to them.

I was in a very strange courtroom. Out of nowhere, referring to me, Weiss burst out, "I think we're all being cowered [*sic*] by this man." Walsh defended, "I'm not being cowered by him. He's not going to cower me." In the middle of a courtroom trial, Weiss told Walsh not to be afraid of me and Walsh responded by telling Weiss that he was not afraid of me at all.

After Weiss finished his questioning of Deana, it was my turn to question her. Deana had stated in her financial statement that she had spent $200 each week for rent, phone, and utilities.

This amount was one-third of her entire claim. I asked, "Mrs. Yalkowsky, you aren't paying rent to anyone, is that correct?" Of course Deana was not paying rent. The house was fully paid for; I paid all the taxes and there was no mortgage.

Deana answered quite honestly, "No, sir."

Walsh, visibly dejected by Deana's answers, said, "I'm going to take a short break." Having seen that Deana's testimony already substantially detracted from her claim for support, Walsh, before leaving the courtroom, directed Deana, "You confer with your attorney."

After Deana had consulted with Weiss, she returned to the witness stand. I then asked her, "Mrs. Yalkowsky, could you please tell us how you arrived at what would come out to over $5,000 a year in vacation and travel. Could you explain how you arrived at that figure?"

Walsh decided that he was not going to take any chances on Deana answering the question. He answered for Deana, saying, "She said she had expenses for cars for their use."

Deana said nothing of the sort; Walsh was testifying for her. I could disprove nothing; it was pointless for me to continue. I said, "I have no further questions."

* * *

The next witness called by Weiss was his ex-partner and Deana's former lawyer, Benjamin Shedler. Weiss asked, "Mr. Shedler, you're an attorney, duly licensed to practice law in the State of New York?"

Shedler replied, "I am."

Weiss continued, "Mr. Shedler, from June of 1978, up until some events that occurred during the course of the trial, did you represent Mrs. Yalkowsky?"

Shedler replied, "Yes, I was in charge of the litigation in our office."

Weiss went on, "From the time you were retained, up through the present time, did you receive any money from Mrs. Yalkowsky?"

Shedler replied, "No, I didn't."

Weiss asked, "Did you receive any disbursements?"

Shedler answered, "I think I received some disbursements to pay for some Examinations Before Trial."

This was the key word: "disbursements." A check paid by Deana to Shedler that I had uncovered and presented to the court would not be called a fee, since it was illegal to accept fees from a client who claimed to be destitute. Instead, the money received by Shedler from Deana would be called a "disbursement." Every payment Shedler received from Deana would be described in that manner.

Weiss did not question Shedler long. I began my own cross-examination of Mr. Shedler. I asked, "Mr. Shedler, you say you received a check that was made out to Deana Yalkowsky from Stanley Yalkowsky for $125?"

Shedler replied, "Yes, sir."

I then asked, "Do you know what it was for?"

Shedler slowly answered, "Because we were going through depositions, Examinations Before Trial, and we needed to pay the court reporter."

When Shedler received the check from Deana, however, there were no depositions, there were no Examinations Before Trial, there was no court reporter. Those procedures did not begin until two months afterward. So

I said, "But, Mr. Shedler, if I tell you that the check was dated August 22, 1978, and the Examination Before Trial was not until October of 1978, that would be impossible, wouldn't it?"

Weiss objected to the question. Walsh, however, proclaimed fatalistically, "If that is a fact, that is a fact."

Shedler tried to regain his composure and said, "I don't know whether it is a fact or not. I haven't got the check before me. I don't know the date of the examination."

Shedler was checkmated in every direction he turned. The Examinations Before Trial did not begin until October 16, 1978. Shedler deposited Deana's check in his account during August of 1978.

There was more. Deana had sworn, in an affidavit prepared for her by Shedler only weeks before the trial began, that she had never paid him anything for disbursements. Shedler needed help—and Walsh provided it. Walsh pronounced, "I'll rule as a matter of law—that is not a legal fee. It is a disbursement." That was the ruling. The most conclusive evidence of Shedler's unlawful receipt of counsel fees received the official endorsement and condonation of a Supreme Court justice's decision. All problems for Shedler were swept away by this one pronouncement.

I then began to question Shedler about his inappropriate conduct in representing Napolitano while he simultaneously represented Deana. I asked him, "Now wasn't there a period from March of 1980 until April of 1980, where you represented Mr. Napolitano and Mrs. Yalkowsky and they both took opposite positions at the same time?"

Walsh made very clear what Shedler's answer would be. Walsh declared, "He didn't represent Napolitano." Walsh decided that this would be Shedler's best defense. Walsh reasoned that Shedler's conduct could be considered improper only if it could be shown that Shedler served as the lawyer for both Deana and Napolitano. Walsh's solution was that Shedler had not been Napolitano's lawyer; another final pronouncement by Judge Walsh. Any proofs I had of Shedler's representation of Napolitano were to be ignored. Even overwhelming proofs, that included another judge's order declaring Shedler was indeed Napolitano's lawyer, would be ignored. All Walsh had to do was to find a new word to describe the relationship. Walsh determined that instead of "representing" Napolitano, Shedler was now merely "appearing" for him.

I continued, "Mr. Shedler, you heard the defendant state that she had $3,000 or some dollars, at the People's Bank, is that correct?"

Shedler replied, "I think so."

Weiss was crestfallen by Shedler's answer. Why did Shedler have to admit to hearing Deana testify that she had money? All Shedler had to do was simply to lie. Walsh was there to protect them. If there were accounts, Walsh would find no accounts. There was no need for Shedler to embarrass Walsh by reverting to truthful answers.

Weiss interjected, "Your Honor, may I just say, having gone through the record, there was no such testimony by Mrs. Yalkowsky, and this is obviously a trick or ploy by Mr. Yalkowsky." Weiss contradicted the testimony of Benjamin Shedler, his own witness.

I stated, "There is testimony by Mrs. Yalkowsky."

Weiss responded, "I defy you to prove it."

I immediately turned to the page where Deana was questioned about her account at People's Bank for Savings, and read the testimony, which had Deana's firm admission that she withdrew $3,297.35 from that bank.

Walsh made his expected pronouncement. He stated rhetorically, "What does that prove? That is her statement, and that is his statement. This is a question of credibility." Such was the way Walsh would protect Shedler and Weiss: to make the indisputable disputable. He would disregard admissions and evidence.

Deana's bank withdrawal slip

Deana's Assets

The court record of the following day's proceedings read, "Whereupon at this time December 16, 1981, the trial of this action continued, and the following ensued." Walsh said, "Mr. Shedler advised me that he was snowbound. Can we go ahead with Mrs. Yalkowsky?"

I replied, "I will be happy to."

Deana returned to the witness stand. I then proceeded to question her about her sworn statements to the court that resulted in her obtaining support and counsel's fees. I asked, "Mrs. Yalkowsky, you filed an affidavit before the court on July 12, 1978, is that correct?"

Deana replied, "Yes."

I then said, "You stated, 'I am utterly without funds of any kind. I must perforce make this application for counsel fees to enable me to defend myself.' Is that correct?"

Deana replied, "That is correct."

I then asked, "Well, do you have an account at Scarsdale National Bank in which you deposited $750 on June 1, 1978?"

Deana answered, "Yes, I opened up an account at the Scarsdale National Bank."

Deana had at least a dozen bank accounts and three safety deposit boxes. Deana's accounts, that were listed and presented to Judge Walsh, included:

> *Scarsdale National Bank*
> *Account number 302-0192401* $ 20,506.00
> *May 15, 1979*
>
> *Scarsdale National Bank*
> *Account number 301-0060701* $106,809.39
> *December 28, 1978*

DEANA'S ASSETS

Scarsdale National Bank
Account number 302-0191855 $ 3,234.69
November 28, 1978

Scarsdale National Bank
Account number 302-0037406 $ 750.00
June 1, 1978

Scarsdale National Bank
Account number 302-187401 $ 586.77
July 12, 1978

Scarsdale National Bank
Account number 2-13745   *Amount unknown*
date unknown

Scarsdale National Bank
Account number 02-14032   *Amount unknown*
date unknown

National Bank of North America
Account number 1364-00290-6 $ 2,306.25
April 27, 1978

National Bank of North America
Account number 974325620 $ 800.00
June 2, 1977

National Bank of North America
Account number K364801509 $ 7,006.20
December 31, 1977

Peoples Bank for Savings
Account number H10118 $ 3,297.35

Citibank
Account number 203535145 $ 500.00
July 26, 1978

National Bank of North America
Vault, opening date,
August 8, 1977   *Amount unknown*

Union Savings Bank
Vault, opening date,
January 15, 1977   *Amount unknown*

National Bank of Westchester
Vault, opening date,
July 28, 1978   *Amount unknown*

Deana obviously had assets. Her financial affidavit, however, which was in Judge Walsh's hands, swore that she had no assets of any kind: no cash, no savings, no securities, no interest in any business, and no income from any other source. Deana swore that she was "completely dependent on the charity and assistance of members of her family."

* * *

Deana was unfathomable. Thinking back, I remember how she would smile and charm a storekeeper into giving her special attention and privilege, and then, much to my amazement, be angry at the storekeeper for favoring her over others. She thought this terribly unjust. The storekeepers and those who bestowed favors upon her never suspected how she felt. She hated them; she enticed them and then hated them.

I never knew anyone like Deana, but the historian Herodotus, writing in the fifth century B.C., described someone who did think and act like her—Amasis, a high-ranking official who eventually became Pharaoh of Egypt. Amasis had the oddest pastime. Whenever he was not busy with his official duties, he spent his time prowling and stealing. Occasionally he would be arrested for these crimes and taken before judges, but once they recognized who he was he was almost always immediately released. As a result when Amasis came to the throne he had a very low opinion of the judges who had acquitted him;

but the few "who had convicted him, he held in the highest honor."

I asked Deana, "In fact, on November 23, 1979, did you not withdraw $3,234.69 from the Scarsdale National Bank?"

Deana replied, "I recall it."

Everything Walsh and Weiss tried, failed. If they claimed Deana had no assets, Deana produced assets. If they argued that she spent the money for her children, Deana would testify, with supporting proofs, that she had transferred monies or given them to Napolitano. It was diabolical. When they claimed Napolitano was a figment of my imagination, in order to prove I was insane and to discredit me, miraculously, almost on the very eve of their success, spitefully and unaccountably, Deana married Napolitano.

I continued my questioning. "Mrs. Yalkowsky, you didn't list in any of these financial affidavits, either in 1980 or 1981, that fact that you had funds, either at the Scarsdale National Bank or the People's Bank for Savings?"

Deana replied, "I didn't."

I then asked the question that was most painful to Walsh and Weiss, I asked Deana, "But you did have these accounts, is that correct?"

Walsh scolded me, saying, "You're confusing us on the dates." There was nothing confusing; the question was straight to the point.

I continued, "Mrs. Yalkowsky, did you have any other account at the Scarsdale National Bank?"

Weiss tried to obscure my question, saying, "Wait, wait, Your Honor. I don't know what item he's referring to." Weiss was pleading with Judge Walsh to stop Deana from answering.

Walsh did better. He answered for Deana, saying, "The question was whether there was any prior transfers and she said she didn't report them, and she had no accounts."

That was not what Deana had said. Deana said she had accounts. Walsh said she had no accounts.

I continued, "Mrs. Yalkowsky, when you claimed that you had no funds of any kind, did you also state you had no credit cards?"

Deana answered, "I have no credit card."

I then produced the records of Deana's use of her American Express card, saying to her, "Mrs. Yalkowsky, I show you this piece of paper. Could you look at it and see if you recognize these items?"

Deana exclaimed, "I recognize this."

I asked Deana, "Mrs. Yalkowsky, did you make certain charges to Econo Car for $202.26...and to A La Carte for $19.42?"

Deana replied, "I can explain that. I believe that was the joint American Express card that we had."

Deana possessed an American Express card in her name; she signed it, used it, acknowledged it, and owned it. Walsh had already granted Deana a money judgment against me based on her sworn declaration that she never had or used an American Express card. Now Deana was tormenting Walsh by admitting she had lied.

Walsh was so chagrined at Deana's answers that he tried to suggest that Deana never previously denied owning or using an American Express card. In a doubting tone, he asked me, "Where is that in the transcript?"

I replied, "Page 2414."

I began to read that portion of the transcript of Deana's earlier testimony where, when Deana was asked if she used an American Express card, she replied, "I never used it. I didn't endorse it either."

Walsh sheepishly said, "Mr. Yalkowsky, you have all of this in the record. Why are you repeating it?"

I answered, "You just asked for it, Your Honor, here she denied it, and now I show it."

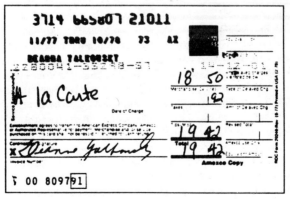

Deana's American Express charges

It is difficult for anyone, lawyer or layman, to believe what followed, and had I not had the official transcript nobody would have believed me. Walsh did not want me to ask Deana any questions pertinent to the case. If I did ask any question that was relevant or meaningful, Walsh proceeded to stop Deana from answering. When I began to ask, "Mrs. Yalkowsky, can you tell us what was spent?" I was not allowed to complete the question. Walsh interrupted, "That is irrelevant."

I said to Walsh, "We're on the issue of finances and I'm asking a direct question on finances, Your Honor, and it is very relevant."

Walsh answered, "I'm not going to take it."

I tried in yet another manner to show that Deana's claim of destitution was untrue. Deana had three separate telephones at her 8 Dell Road premises. I tried to show that the telephone bills were very large, hundreds of dollars a month, and that Deana even used aliases in her attempt to hide the assets she had to pay for these bills. It was during my questioning of Deana about these telephone bills that Walsh lost control of himself.

It happened when I asked Deana, "Mrs. Yalkowsky, under the name of Deana Saynor, telephone number 742-5039, does this telephone company record, listing you as secretary to Greenlawn and showing the bill for $161 and some cents, sent to 8 Dell Road, is this an accurate and true representation?" The question had everything in it—Deana's alias, her connection with Greenlawn, her paying large telephone bills.

Walsh screamed at me, "Mr. Yalkowsky, certainly this is not a bill. I see telephone bills every month. This doesn't look like a bill to me."

Weiss whined, "It is like he calls everything else, what he wants to call it. He's ascertained that that is a bill, and perjury is perjury and fraud is fraud, and he's the only one guilty of fraud throughout the trial."

Walsh, staring at the telephone bill in his hand, then said, "I rule that is not a bill and therefore she can't testify as to a bill if it's not a bill."

I resumed questioning Deana about her Greenlawn Landscaping Company account at Scarsdale National Bank. Weiss objected to my questioning.

Walsh asked, "What do they show?"

I explained, "They show the defendant's control of vast amounts of money and assets."

Walsh responded, "I'll sustain the objection. They're only transcripts of an account. They aren't checks. We don't know who they went to or who they came from."

I said, "Your Honor—" I wanted to explain that I had the checks that showed Deana's control of Greenlawn Landscaping Company, and knew where they went and from whom they came. I was not permitted to complete my sentence.

Walsh said, "I have made the ruling, Mr. Yalkowsky. Please get along."

I had over a hundred pages of documents that proved Deana had a controlling interest in the Greenlawn Landscaping Company. I had Visa card and telephone company records evidencing Deana's connection with Greenlawn Landscaping Company, as well as payroll records. I had bank transcripts that showed that, by the end of December 1977, the Greenlawn Landscaping Company account had a balance of $52,265.28 which by the end of December 1978, had grown to $106,809.35. I had transcripts that showed that the account generated millions of dollars in activity each year. I had documents that showed that Deana was the President of the Greenlawn Landscaping Company and had signed checks for that corporation; this evidence was before the court. Walsh declared, "I decline it."

I then tried another line of questioning. How could Deana plead financial poverty while, at the same time, check into very expensive hotels? Walsh saw no purpose in my questioning Deana about this topic.

I thought that there was a purpose and asked Judge Walsh, "May I ask how she paid for the Plaza Hotel?"

Walsh answered, "What difference?"

I responded to Walsh, saying, "You really feel that it doesn't make any difference?"

Walsh replied, "It is remote, so remote that it does not have anything to do with her present situation."

Walsh and Weiss had already decided what they had to do; they spoke between themselves. When it seemed their conversation had ended, Walsh turned to me and said, "I gave you an opportunity for any defenses as to why you didn't pay. I haven't heard a word on it."

At that moment, I did wish Walsh was dead. I could not control these thoughts; the years of misery and pain that had been inflicted upon me, my father's death, my children's spiritual death, and this terrible judge saying that he had not heard a word from me expressing why I opposed paying Deana and her lawyers provoked these thoughts. Weiss added his own taunt, saying, "There is no proof, there is no testimony, only his delusion. I defy him to produce any evidence, and he hasn't done it. He's made charges and countercharges and he hasn't produced one piece of evidence."

I asked Deana, "Could you tell us how much you spent in 1979 for your children for food and clothing?" Walsh stopped me. I tried to reason with Walsh again, saying,

"If I show you, Your Honor, that there is a source of income..."

Walsh interrupted, "To feed the children?"

I replied, "To do anything."

Weiss interjected, "If he can show his plan in starving out this family, because she's alive and the children are alive, to him there is something wrong. I say any man who uses these tactics shouldn't be called a human person."

Walsh, who had interviewed the children only a week before and had already announced that nothing like that had ever happened, now replied to Weiss, "Thank God they have eaten."

Weiss said, "He didn't give them a dime and they ate."

Walsh responded, "He's admitted that."

Weiss drooled, "He would be happy if they starve."

My questioning of Deana confirmed that she made a false claim when she swore that I left her in 1978 without giving her a penny for support. I established this fact simply by asking her, "Mrs. Yalkowsky, on November 15, 1978, do you recall stating here, 'He has just sent me some postdated checks for the next several weeks, and each check is in the amount of $200.'"

Deana replied, "Yes." It was that simple. Deana admitted that I supported her in 1978.

I said to Judge Walsh, "They made motions and applications and stated that I left my wife without giving a dime, and have not supported my wife and children for four years." The "they" included Walsh himself; he too had made this very claim.

Walsh defended, "Nobody said that."

Walsh was trying to withdraw the statements he had repeatedly made throughout the trial, to make what he was now saying consistent with the evidence in front of him—checks that proved I supported Deana.

I asked Deana, "Mrs. Yalkowsky, I show you these checks which are support checks that I claim to have given you. Would you look at them and see if you have received all of these checks in support payments?"

Weiss, seeing the checks in front of his eyes and having heard Walsh already concede that the checks had been received by Deana, decided at that moment to withdraw his repeated claim that I had left Deana without providing support.

The day's hearing came to a close. Walsh said to Weiss, "Have Mr. Shedler here at 9:30 tomorrow morning and we'll proceed at that time."

That evening, when I returned to my apartment, I received welcome news. Thomas Kavanaugh of Scarsdale National Bank had been properly subpoenaed; he would be required to testify the next day, December 17, 1981.

The next morning, the roads having been cleared of snow, Shedler was able to return to the court. Walsh began the proceedings by saying, "All right, Mr. Shedler, you're already sworn, and you will continue to testify." I asked Shedler what it was that made him conclude that I should not be able to see my children.

Shedler explained, "You were harassing the children. You were filling their ears with statements that their mother was no good, that she was a tramp. You even called her a whore to the children's faces. The children got hysterical. The children didn't want to visit with you and I felt that it was improper from the point of view of the health and welfare of the children, that they see you, and that was my opinion, that is what I told you. That is what I told your attorney."

I then asked, "Mr. Shedler, all these things that you

heard about me, you never saw any of these things, did you, that you just related?"

Shedler answered, "Some of the things I knew of my own knowledge. Some of the things were told to me by my client, and I may have gotten some of the information from the children themselves."

I said to Shedler, "We have what you got from your client; could you tell us what information you got from elsewhere concerning your coming to a decision that it was best that the children not see their father?"

Shedler answered, "You didn't support the children." Shedler was still making the claim that Walsh and Weiss had already abandoned when they admitted that I had supported the children.

Shedler continued, "And you certainly weren't entitled to badger them, and to continue to harass them."

I then asked Shedler, "Do you have any other way of knowing about harassing other than Mrs. Yalkowsky telling you?"

Shedler's face grew pale. He sat with his hands holding his chin, for literally minutes, groping to think of some other source for his being so convinced that I had harassed and badgered my children.

I interjected, "Let the record reflect that Mr. Shedler is thinking long and hard."

Shedler finally blurted out, "I say primarily from Mrs. Yalkowsky."

I continued my questioning, asking, "Mr. Shedler, you claimed you haven't received any fees from Mrs. Yalkowsky, is that correct?"

Shedler replied, "Yes, sir."

I continued, "And you claim for three years or four years, however long you represented her, she had no funds?"

Shedler replied, "That's right."

I then asked, "Mr. Shedler, you already were submitted documents that she had accounts at Citibank, accounts at Scarsdale National Bank, and you still felt that she couldn't pay you?"

Shedler answered, "These were all your statements. She denied that it was her accounts. You couldn't prove it either."

Shedler heard Deana admit to having these accounts. I stressed this to Walsh. Walsh responded, "Whether he believes it or not is what you're driving at; that is not his obligation to evaluate that."

Walsh had to maintain that position for himself. This would enable him later to rule that Deana had no assets, that the lawyers were never paid, that Deana didn't receive support payments, and that Deana had no accounts. In fact, Walsh could determine anything he wished by deciding to believe or disbelieve whatever he wished.

I then proceeded to question Shedler about an affidavit he filed which stated that none of the Greenlawn Landscaping Company checks went to Mrs. Yalkowsky. I asked him, "Isn't that perjury or fraud or some kind of crime?"

Shedler did not know what to say. He struggled for words, answering incoherently, "As I recall the testimony, Mr. Napolitano said that perhaps a dozen checks went into the account. He didn't say that she got the money. He said they went into her account."

That Concludes the Case

Allen Weiss took the witness stand. His testimony was given to establish that he was entitled to receive from me a substantial sum of money, based on New York State Law which requires a husband to pay the legal fees of destitute wife in a matrimonial action.

I asked Weiss if he had heard the testimony concerning Deana's account at Scarsdale National Bank. Weiss did not answer; he just repeated my question, saying, "Did I hear the testimony in this court?" I tried again, asking, "Did you review the testimony?" Weiss again did not answer; he repeated my question, again saying, "Did I hear the testimony in this case?" I saw that Weiss had no intention of answering my question and that Walsh certainly did not want the question answered, so I moved on.

I then asked Weiss, "Did you review the testimony that indicated that Mrs. Yalkowsky had an account at the People's Savings Bank?"

Weiss objected and Walsh agreed with him, saying, "That is not the issue here. That is back several years ago."

With that statement, Walsh terminated my questioning of Weiss. I had to say again, "Your Honor, I can't go any further."

Walsh then said, "Okay, fine, that will conclude the testimony then." I had only finished with Weiss, however; there was more to be heard. There was also the Scarsdale National Bank's testimony. But Walsh's expression meant all testimony was over, not just Weiss's. Everything was over. I exclaimed rhetorically, "I can't believe it."

Walsh had decided he was not going to hear another word. Deana's testimony had made him sick, and now Weiss was testifying in a way that was disturbing him. Walsh decided he had had enough. He said, "That concludes the case."

Weiss and I stood in stunned amazement. There was no question in my mind that Weiss was just as shocked as I to see Walsh run from the bench. We did not move. Ron DeSilva, the stenographer, did not move, nor did the court attendant. We all stood there in silence, thinking perhaps that Walsh would return. Weiss and I even walked back into the little corridor behind the courtroom that led to Judge Walsh's chambers to see if he was returning. We then came back to the courtroom, asking ourselves and the court officer if the trial was really over. We waited in that court room for no less than ten minutes, but Walsh did not return. The stenographic record of the court proceedings read:

Whereupon, at this time, the trial of the action was concluded.

Certified to be a true and correct transcript of the within trial. Ronald DeSilva, C.S.R. R.P.R., Official Court Reporter.

Walsh's Decision

The very next day I called Henry Neale, Jr., Scarsdale National Bank's lawyer.

Neale: You called me?

Yalkowsky: Yes, Mr. Neale. I subpoenaed the records for the trial on Kavanaugh. He got the subpoena but he didn't come.

Neale: Well, the trial is over so what difference does it make? It was too late; you asked for stuff that we couldn't produce in that time. In any event, Mr. Yalkowsky, your trial is over. I went up there finally at three o'clock, was prepared to make a motion to quash and the judge said forget it. The trial is over, so we can't worry about that anymore.

Yalkowsky: Did you see the judge?

Neale: Did I see him? No, I talked to someone.

Yalkowsky: And you don't want to produce those records?

Neale: No.

The following evening I spoke to Ronald DeSilva, the court reporter.

Yalkowsky: The judge said he will get back to me.

DeSilva: But we never got back to you. You know, the transcript, when you read it somebody will be looking, oh, there must be a page missing over there because Yalkowsky hasn't got back on the stand, you were both dumbfounded. When you have both sides dumbfounded, you come out amazed. I mean, you

are not the only one amazed over here.
Everybody involved is amazed.

Five months later, on May 18, 1982, Judge Walsh rendered his decision. He granted Deana's lawyers $50,000 for their services, awarded Deana $34,500, on the basis of her claimed destitution, and left the custody condition just as it was, which, in effect, denied me access to my children.

The next day, after Walsh signed the formal order granting Shedler and Weiss their award, Weiss sent legal documents known as restraining notices to every bank I had accounts in, ordering them to withhold from me any money to which I was entitled. As a result, my entire economic life was stopped; I could not write a check.

A week later I visited the Appellate Division, seeking to ask that court to delay the enforcement of Walsh's decision until I had a chance to appeal it. I also wanted to ask them to stop the restraining orders, which were crushing me. Irving Selkin, the Appellate Division's ever-present clerk, told me, when I arrived there, that, since no judge was around, I should leave the papers with him and that he would call me the next day.

Selkin did call me the next day to tell me that a delay would be granted if I posted a bond for $35,000 with the court by the following Monday morning. I told Selkin that, while I had the money, I could not withdraw it from the bank because all my accounts were restrained. Selkin told me to hold on while he explained my dilemma to Judge Guy Mangano. He then returned to tell me that the court's decision was final. I would have to post a bond for $35,000 even though, as the conditions now stood, it would be impossible for me do so. Selkin, however, added that a private meeting could be arranged for me to see Judge Mangano personally, but that it would be best not to talk about what could be done for me over the telephone.

On June 29, 1982, after I refused to meet privately with Judge Mangano, my request seeking to release the restraints on my accounts was denied.

I wrote directly to Justice Milton Mollen, the Chief Justice of the Appellate Division. I informed him of the criminal conduct occurring before Judge Walsh and the Appellate Division. My charges were explicit. I urged that the matter be referred to the Brooklyn office of the District Attorney for investigation.

Mollen wrote back to me, "I assure you that the justices of this court decide the matters presented to them solely on the merits. I find no basis to conduct an investigation...."

In desperation I appealed hopelessly to anybody and everybody, writing everywhere of the court's misconduct. Elizabeth Holtzman of the Kings County District Attorney's office wrote back to me:

> *This office is precluded from prosecution... Charges of judicial misconduct are handled by the Commission on Judicial Conduct.*

Patrick F.Y. Mulhearn, Counsel to Mayor Koch, wrote to me:

> *Copies of your letter have been forwarded to the state Commission of Judicial Conduct...The Mayor has full confidence in the propriety and judiciousness of the Commission findings.*

I even called Stanley Friedman, who had replaced Patrick Cunningham and was now the Bronx Democratic party leader. Friedman thought my charges of court corruption were unbelievable; he too recommended that I forward my complaints of court corruption to the Judicial Conduct Commission.

Futilely I wrote again to the Judicial Conduct Commission, reiterating my request that they tell me what it was that Judge Walsh had said in his defense that prompted them to dismiss the charges I brought against him. Robert Tembeckjian, the clerk of the Judicial Conduct Commission, in a tone of sympathetic annoyance, responded:

> Each time, the Commission had the benefit of all the material you submitted...I appreciate your disappointment in the Commission's decision, as I believe you appreciate the time both the Commission and the staff have devoted in response to your numerous letters and telephone calls.

Tembeckjian then proceeded to correct the grammar I used in my letter by stating that I was a "complainant" and not a "plaintiff." He then explained to me that a judge's response is secret and not open to public view. Therefore, he said, I would not be told what Judge Walsh had said in his defense nor would I be given the opportunity to dispute what he said. My protestations that this procedure was unfair were scoffed at by Tembeckjian, who informed me that a complainant making a charge against a judge is never entitled to hear a judge's response, nor entitled to know what evidence the Commission considered in evaluating the charges brought against a judge.

ENEMY OF
THE JUDGES

State Courts

All the while I had been sending the Departmental Disciplinary Committee evidence of Shedler's, Weiss's and Kozupsky's misconduct.

I had, over the years, thought of the Departmental Disciplinary Committee as irreproachable and of such high integrity that it seemed a matter of chance whether I, or other lawyers, could go through our years of practice safe from the high-minded scrutiny of that somber body of overseer lawyers, who demanded nothing less than absolute honesty from every attorney practicing law in their jurisdiction.

My mid-1981 complaint to the Disciplinary Committee directed charges of misconduct at each of the lawyers of the firm made up of Benjamin Shedler, Allen Weiss, Allen Kozupsky, and Mark Zafrin. I complained of perjury, fraud, subornation of perjury, and other acts committed by them that were criminal in nature. Every claim I made was supported by documentary evidence.

When Shedler, Weiss and Kozupsky submitted a claim for counsel fees and obtained those fees from me, based on their sworn claim that their client, my ex-wife, was penniless and on the verge of welfare; when they knew that she was not penniless but of vast wealth; and when they saw the evidence and heard the testimony of her wealth, which was confirmed by bank officials and handwriting experts and even her own testimony, they committed fraud.

Shedler's reply to the Disciplinary Committee did not respond to the charges I made in my complaint. I called his nonresponse to the attention of the Committee; I received no answer from them.

In despair, I visited the Departmental Disciplinary Committee and met with Joseph Rosenberg, who was assigned to the matter. I immediately saw that something was wrong. Rosenberg was adversarial, side-glancing. I sensed trouble. Rosenberg was working against me; I could feel it. At this time I had no idea why a Departmental Disciplinary Committee staff member should be working against me.

I did not appreciate, as yet, the difficulty I had created for the Disciplinary Committee. Not only were they put in a position where, if they found Shedler guilty of misconduct, they would have to find Judge Walsh a co-conspirator; in addition, of necessity, they would have to find Milton Mollen, the Presiding Justice of the Appellate Division, a co-conspirator of equal guilt as well.

In desperation at the Departmental Disciplinary Committee's refusal to perform its duties, I sued the law firm of Shedler, Weiss and Kozupsky in the Supreme Court, charging them with fraud.

Judge Benjamin Altman dismissed the action I brought against Weiss and Kozupsky, but not against Shedler. He could not dismiss my action against Shedler—not when Shedler admitted to my charges of fraud, and claimed that his partners committed fraud as well.

I asked Judge Altman to review his dismissal of my action against Weiss and Kozupsky, since Shedler had implicated them. My request did not reach Altman. Instead, Judge Thomas Galligan, who had previously been investigated for purchasing his judgeship, appeared out of nowhere, usurped my requests for review designated to be presented only to Judge Altman, and dismissed my entire complaint—this time including Benjamin Shedler in the dismissal.

Despite Benjamin Shedler's confession of fraud, the Appellate Division, First Department, when they heard the matter on appeal, endorsed Judge Galligan's decision. So did the Court of Appeals.

Once it became clear to the controlling elements of the judiciary that I was their enemy, they dismissed almost every action I brought, no matter how correct it was.

I brought an action against Judge Walsh and District Attorney Jonathan Friedman.

The section of the action I brought against Judge Walsh requested a hearing to determine whether Walsh had exceeded his authority in the exercise of his judicial duties. Judge Edward Greenfield was the judge assigned to the matter. Greenfield was presented with the evidence of how Judge Walsh knowingly suppressed trial testimony and obstructed justice, and of how Walsh knowingly lied to a jury and encouraged disobedience of court orders. Judge Greenfield ruled that this was all proper.

The other section of my action involved Jonathan Friedman, the former Assistant District Attorney of Westchester County, who had turned over my complaint and confidential evidence to Judge Walsh. Judge Arthur Blynn determined that Jonathan Friedman had acted properly when he provided Judge Walsh with evidence that incriminated him and also acted properly when he relied upon the judge to decide whether he should be prosecuted or not.

* * *

There was one short interval of time, however, when legally correct decisions were granted to me by the courts. On December 6, 1982, the Appellate Division, Second Department, reversed Judge Walsh's decision which granted Deana the house on Dell Road, and returned the house to me.

The Appellate Division's decision was made just weeks after I had written a letter to Gerald Stern, the Administrator of the Judicial Conduct Commission, and to numerous judges of the New York State courts. This letter and its contents, particularly as it related to court corruption, had a more profound effect than I had estimated.

Allen Weiss could not help but refer to that letter, when he bitterly petitioned the Appellate Division to review its decision that reversed Judge Walsh, saying:

> Mr. Yalkowsky is attempting to intimidate the court. Indeed the tone, tenor and style of the Stern letter leads to the conclusion that he is bereft of all rationality and reason. His false, vituperative, and vile accusations against Judge William Walsh, Jr., the Appellate Division justices, Justice Milton Mollen, Irving Selkin and a host of others are as incredible and unworthy of belief as was his trial testimony and the evidence he offered.

My good fortune with the Appellate Division, Second Department, continued until April 11, 1983, when that court rendered yet another decision that was favorable to me. The decision required that the Scarsdale National Bank provide me with detailed information it possessed of Deana's accounts, as well as subject itself to a hearing to determine whether it be held in contempt.

The decision was so much in my favor that I thought a major change had occurred. It appeared that the Appellate Division judges were now ready to recognize that Scarsdale National Bank had engaged in fraudulent conduct and that accounts maintained at that bank had been deliberately suppressed and not "harmlessly" lost.

As I would later learn, the decision was not popularly received. There were strong rumblings that the only reason the Appellate Division, Second Department, made its decision in my favor was because of the conduct of Scarsdale National Bank's lawyer, J. Henry Neale, Jr., whose false affidavits, so blatantly submitted to the courts, embarrassed and compromised the judges. Neale had to be removed.

J. Henry Neale, Jr., was replaced by Theodore Steingut, son of the powerful politician Stanley Steingut. The justices of the Appellate Division were greatly relieved; they felt far more comfortable with young Steingut, whose father and grandfather were politicians they had known so well.

Within days of becoming the lawyer for Scarsdale National Bank, Theodore Steingut was at my apartment, sitting with me in my living room. In addition to visiting me, Steingut contacted friends and acquaintances of mine in his efforts to learn as much as he could about me.

Steingut, in a sense, was informally "hired" by the Appellate Division judges for the purpose of determining who I was. Steingut could happily report back to them that I was nobody for them to worry about. As a result of Steingut's investigation, the Appellate Division judges determined that nothing would be given to me and that what was already given would be taken back.

The Appellate Division's method for revoking their own order was first to have Scarsdale National Bank disobey the order, and then, when I tried to enforce the original order, simply deny my request—a remarkable maneuver. The justices of the Appellate Division had successfully cheated me.

The courts were almost limitless in the ways they devised to harm me. One method they frequently used was to simply and arbitrarily change the laws whenever it suited them. For instance, the rule of the court which required that orders of judges that were not obeyed be returned to the same judge who issued the original order was no longer in effect if and when I was one of the litigants. As a result, lawyers adverse to me were not discouraged or disheartened when decisions were not in their favor; all they had to do was ask for whatever they wanted over and over again until judges such as Thomas Galligan, Herbert Altman, Martin Rettinger, and Edward Greenfield would finally be found to rule in their behalf.

When Donald Goldberg, one of the lawyers associated with the Shedler, Weiss and Kozupsky firm, asked the court for a ruling in his favor, and his request was denied by Justice Seymour Schwartz, Goldberg simply made the same request again. This time, instead of it being heard by Judge Schwartz as the court rules required, Goldberg had the matter referred to the judge of his choice, Justice Edward Greenfield, who enthusiastically granted his request.

Shedler, Weiss, and Kozupsky used the same tactic, ignoring denials and repeatedly making the same requests until matters were finally referred to the judges of their choice, who would then invariably rule in their favor.

The results of these tactics were disastrous to me. In September of 1982, Weiss and Kozupsky asked a judge to order my commodity seat sold. They did not mention that the same request had been denied by another judge only two days before. Allen Weiss presented his request to the new judge, falsely stating "No previous application has been made for this relief to any court or judge thereof." As a result, my seat on the Commodity Exchange was sold.

My Realization

I was tired and worn and sick from it all, and I was hurting. I could speak to no one but Peree. No one understood. Everyone advised that I should give it all up, run away if necessary, start all over again. Accept my loss. Everyone was sensible and practical, and I appeared so unbending and inflexible. But I *did* want to run away. I did want to stop. I wanted to enjoy my days and nights. I longed for a beach to lie on, ocean water to wash me ashore, friends to laugh with, a woman close to me. But just when the thought of ending the struggle was about to take hold of me and I was ready to surrender, I had a realization.

I was home in my room. It was some months after the trial. Peree was in her room. I just started calling "Peree," louder and louder. Peree was worried as she came running to me, wondering why I was calling her so loudly; she was not that far away from me. It was then that I told her of my realization.

It was that Deana was with me, always with me, with her whole heart and being, and suffering no less than I. She loved and missed Peree and Larin. She was heartbroken at keeping Irina and Risah from me. She mourned my father and missed my mother. She could not bear being with Napolitano, and, more than anything else, she wanted justice. Our purpose was the same. She had to do whatever she did in the way she did; it was the only way.

Deana hated injustice. Her feelings, however, were not something she could discuss with me. I would not have understood. She knew though what was in me—and knew how to bring it out of me. As soon as this realization entered into my being, confirmation of its truth came almost immediately.

In the summer of 1982, Deana resumed her love and motherhood of Peree.

* * *

There never was a defense presented to my complaints. Never did Shedler, Weiss, Henry Neale, Jr., nor any of the other attorneys I charged with fraud and misconduct, respond directly to my charges. There was only one opposition argument: that I had dared to charge the judiciary with corruption—and that was enough. Judges, lawyers, and courts, upon hearing what I had said, immediately united in opposition to me. My claims of court corruption were stressed as if the mere fact that I made such claims was sufficient in and of itself to dismiss anything I presented.

Allen Weiss knew just what to say when he stated to Judge Altman on May 19, 1982:

> *The obviously deranged attack upon Justice William A. Walsh of Westchester County, the Disciplinary Committee, the Scarsdale National Bank, the District Attorney of Westchester, are clearly relevant considerations for this court.*

Robert Sussman, Kenneth Horwitz, and every lawyer in opposition to me saw the value of stressing my claims of court corruption. It brought them the instant friendship and protection of the courts. Sussman, representing Irving Bank Corporation, on June 30, 1982, stated:

> *Plaintiff has attacked the entire State Supreme Court in Westchester, the Westchester District Attorney, the Appellate Division, and the Judicial Conduct Committee.*

Even my former attorney Richard Friedman, when confronted with documentary evidence that he had stolen over $10,000 from me, had the perspicacity to defend himself in the same manner.

I learned of Friedman's theft early in 1983 when I wrote to the Westchester County Clerk's office asking them to return the $10,000 that I had posted as a bond. The information I received was that the $10,000 I had deposited with the court, plus interest, had already been picked up by my attorneys, Friedman and Levy.

I wrote for further information. In the correspondence that followed, I received a copy of a check for $10,387.93 made payable to me and endorsed by me.

There was one major problem: the check had not been endorsed by me. My signature had been forged and the check deposited in the account of Richard Friedman and his partner, Robert Levy.

Although I was not totally shocked to learn that Richard Friedman had stolen from me, I still doubted that he would actually do such a thing. After all, he had already received over $200,000 in fees from me. I checked the facts thoroughly, to make certain. It was certain.

I complained to the Departmental Disciplinary Committee. On December 13, 1983, Richard Friedman sent his reply to the Disciplinary Committee. He did not attempt to refute my charges. Friedman simply stated, referring to me:

> He had made a complaint against the trial judge, Judge Walsh, alleging he was either corrupt or incompetent. Mr. Yalkowsky may have made additional broad stroked allegations against other members of the judiciary, perhaps relating to the Appellate Division judges themselves.

That was all Friedman had to say. My charges against him had to be dismissed. Just as the Disciplinary

Committee protected Phillip Dondi, who aided the judges in their battle against Maurice Nadjari, they would also protect Richard Friedman in his struggle with me.

Lawyers interconnected with a corrupt judiciary were scrupulously protected by the Departmental Disciplinary Committee. The notorious Roy Cohn, a favorite of the controlling elements of the judiciary, was permitted to commit crime after crime, year after year, without fear of Disciplinary Committee action. The Disciplinary Committee also protected Seymour Kane, allowing him to continue to practice law, even though he had been found guilty of a crime involving an attempt to bribe Judge Burton Roberts. Lawyers, however, whose misconduct did not include sharing proceeds with New York City Supreme Court judges would find themselves disbarred by the Disciplinary Committee for the most minor acts of misconduct.

Tampering With the Cosmos

On January 6, 1983, I learned for the first time that there never had been a Departmental Disciplinary Committee investigation of Benjamin Shedler, Allen Weiss, and Allen Kozupsky. This fact was confirmed by James Cohen, a high-ranking member of the staff of the Disciplinary Committee, who recommended that, instead of my discussing the matter with him, I speak to Martin London, the Chairman of the Departmental Disciplinary Committee; I called Martin London.

London was a highly regarded member of the prestigious law firm of Paul, Weiss, Rifkind, Wharton & Garrison, who had been placed at the head of the Disciplinary Committee. Ostensibly it appeared as if he was an unpaid volunteer, honorably sacrificing his services; in actuality, his position held enormous power. Such strategic positions, whether in the Judicial Conduct Commission or the Departmental Disciplinary Committee, gave their holders incalculable influence. The Paul, Weiss, Rifkind firm had wielded this power for decades.

London instructed me to write him, and I did so on January 10, 1983, outlining to him my complaints against the lawyers, and the improper activities of the Departmental Disciplinary Committee.

After more than a week had passed, and I had received no response to my letter, I called London. He told me he had not as yet read my letter.

After more time had passed and I still had not received a response from London, I wrote to the members of the Disciplinary Committee. This second letter finally prompted London to write back to me:

> *The charges you level are serious and I have asked John Keenan, a member of the Executive*

Committee of this Committee to inquire and report to me on their substance.

I called Keenan, the same John Keenan who was so effective in undermining Maurice Nadjari, but he did not wish to speak to me. He left word with his secretary that he would be meeting with Rosenberg of the Departmental Disciplinary Committee on February 10, 1983, and so there would be no purpose in discussing anything with me until after that meeting took place. This seemed odd. I was the one making the complaint, yet Keenan was not meeting with me but rather with one of the people about whom I complained.

Having no inkling of what Martin London and John Keenan had planned, I called Martin London. I wanted to know why my complaints of the lawyers' fraud, perjury, larceny, and false affidavits had been ignored for the past two years. London avoided my calls.

I soon found out why Keenan was meeting with the people I complained of and why London would not take my calls. Martin London, while lulling me into the belief that an inquiry into my complaint was being made, was stealthily plotting and endorsing the preparation of a Departmental Disciplinary Committee complaint to be brought against me by Appellate Division Justice Milton Mollen. The complaint was designed to warn me that if I continued to make charges of court corruption, I could be disbarred.

A meeting was finally scheduled with John Keenan. Keenan thought that the maneuver of February 10, 1983, which turned his investigation of the Departmental Disciplinary Committee into a complaint by Milton Mollen against me, should now have sufficiently prepared me to discuss compromise. At the meeting, Keenan began by reminding me that a complaint had been logged against me. He asked me what I now wanted. I told him my demands; I insisted on the resignations of Michael Gentile, and Joseph Rosenberg. Keenan winced. My demands gave clear indication that the Disciplinary Committee's plan was not going to succeed. Keenan was extremely uncomfortable. He did not want to view any of the evidence I had brought to show him. He did not want to investigate politically powerful judges and lawyers; not when his appointment to the federal judiciary was only weeks away.

In March of 1983, I complained to the Departmental Disciplinary Committee that Kenneth Horwitz, the attorney for Shedler, Weiss and Kozupsky, had submitted a false affidavit to the court. I provided the Committee with the document. Receiving no answer, I again wrote to the Committee, to inform them that while awaiting their response Kenneth Horwitz had submitted yet another false affidavit to the court.

Receiving no reply, I could not determine whether my complaint against Kenneth Horwitz was being processed. I requested that the Appellate Division order a hearing to find out whether the Departmental Disciplinary Committee was maliciously preventing an investigation of Kenneth Horwitz. The Appellate Division, First Department, which appointed and had full control of the Departmental Disciplinary Committee, denied my request.

What I was facing was unique. I was petitioning the Appellate Division to prevent the abuses of the Departmental Disciplinary Committee, when, for reasons I did not as yet know, it was the Appellate Division itself that was ordering the abuses.

On April 29, 1983, I received a startling explanation to many of my questions. It came quite unexpectedly. It happened while I was discussing one of my appeals before the judges of the Appellate Division, First Department. Suddenly one of them, Judge E. Leo Milonas, arose and announced his disqualification from further deliberations on matters involving myself and my opponents, mumbling that he had a "relationship" with one or more of the attorneys involved in the litigation. When I tried to get some clarification from Milonas, Judge Theodore Kupferman interrupted me to say, "He doesn't have to tell you."

Now I understood why the Departmental Disciplinary Committee ignored my complaints; there were very powerful reasons. Appellate Division Justice E. Leo Milonas was impermissibly related in some way to Shedler, Weiss, Kozupsky, and their attorney Kenneth Horwitz and had already illegally ruled in their favor in a matter that was harmful to me without revealing this interpersonal relationship.

I wrote to Judge Milonas and asked him to explain his relationship with the lawyers. I wrote, "I believe you have a legal responsibility to state whom your relationship was with and the nature of such relationship. I would respectfully appreciate your prompt reply." I received no reply.

Milonas's failure to disqualify himself at an earlier time was surprising even to his colleagues, who would gladly have ruled as he desired, if only he had asked. They were now only too happy to rule in Milonas's behalf after his disqualification.

Judges of the Appellate Divisions almost always recognize each others' desires, especially when to not recognize and respect these desires could lead to retaliation, something they could ill afford; certainly not while they sit side by side day after day. An unwritten law demands of them mutual cooperation and

reciprocation. Too many friends, relatives, and influ
ential politicians appear before them to risk strif
among themselves. Even so, it has always been considere
ill-mannered for a judge to ask too frequently fo
favors from his colleagues.

Milonas made a conscious effort to avoid frequen
impositions on his fellow judges. For a long time h
thought he could rule on the Shedler, Weiss, Kozupsky
and Horwitz matters without anyone knowing of his rela
tionship with them; but when I appeared before him o
April 29, 1983, and for no particular reason fixed m
eyes directly on him, looking at none of the othe
judges, Milonas decided then and there to disquali
himself.

As I expected, on May 3, 1983, the Appellat
Division, First Department, judges, without E. Le
Milonas, ruled against me on my claim that Kennet
Horwitz submitted false affidavits to them.

On June 10, 1983, in legal papers submitted to th
Appellate Division First Department, I said to th
judges rhetorically:

> As the dispensers of justice that is your
> burden, no matter how discomfiting it may be.
> There is enough injustice in the world without
> the participation of judges. Untimely deaths and
> wars and diseases where justice is denied
> without judges. But you who are judges should
> never deny justice. I may be wrong in the long
> run and should not have pursued this course, but
> that is not for you to decide. You have your
> laws as guidance to follow. When you suspend
> laws to make a pragmatic judgment you are
> tampering with the cosmos, not I.

In June of 1983, I wrote to Lawrence McGovern, a
Departmental Disciplinary Committee staff member, asking

him, "As to Allen Weiss, has a complaint file been opened? And if so, when was it opened?" Lawrence McGovern replied:

> The policy of the Disciplinary Committee is to refrain from providing complainants or respondents with either oral or written reports of the status of its investigations or preliminary recommendations or findings. This policy must be strictly adhered to for obvious reasons. It will not be possible, therefore, to provide you with the information requested in your letter....

A few months later, McGovern returned to me the indisputable evidence I submitted to him that proved Kenneth Horowitz had submitted backdated false affidavits to the court on behalf of his clients Benjamin Shedler and Allen Weiss. McGovern, without a word of explanation, wrote to me, "The tape of the conversation, which you forwarded to the Disciplinary Committee, with a letter dated July 5, 1983, is returned to you herewith."

I hoped that somewhere, the higher we went, there was a place above reproach. I thought perhaps I could find justice in the federal courts.

The corrupt trail that started in a Westchester Supreme Court and wound its way into the state Appellate Courts had also taken me into the Federal courts.

Federal Courts

My first venture into the Federal court began in the middle of 1982. I worked extremely hard to prepare a detailed complaint; I had to: I was suing numerous lawyers, judges, and bank officials, as well as district attorneys and other high officials.

Soon after my suit began, I received a telephone call from Federal Court Judge Thomas Griesa's law clerk, who said to me,

> *My name is Kerry Konrad and I am the law clerk for Judge Griesa. I would like to set up a conference. I think we can have a conference which will be fruitful for us—for you and at least for those that we could get—and we wouldn't dispose of the action at that time.*

Judge Griesa's law clerk told me there would be a conference on October 4, 1982; he said that one of the lawyers, Kenneth Horwitz, who represented Shedler, Weiss, and Kozupsky, had arranged to have this conference. Konrad assured me that my complaint would not be dismissed. The conference, he told me, was only for the purpose of clarification. It seemed a reasonable request; I had been called personally by a Federal judge's law clerk.

On October 4, 1982, with my daughter, I came to Judge Griesa's conference room. Several lawyers for the defense were there as well. After only seconds had passed, Judge Griesa stood up and announced that though he had not read my complaint he was nevertheless dismissing it.

I was astounded. I said to Judge Griesa, "May I respond, Your Honor?"

He replied, "Yes."

I said, "Considering that Your Honor just stated that

he didn't read the document, I would think that would be somewhat unfair."

Judge Griesa replied, "I'll be frank with you. I don't intend to read it...this would take hours to read and figure out. It is not my burden to do that."

When Griesa announced that my matter was dismissed, it was a sight to behold: a dozen lawyers came charging out into the corridor, shaking hands and congratulating one another. I looked at Peree and she at me, as we all gathered in the elevator to make our way out of the court. Horwitz and the other lawyers were smiling with satisfaction. The floor-by-floor descent was accompanied by their laughter and stares of scorn.

I wrote to Judge Griesa and stated that I was appealing his decision; I told him that I had served another and different complaint. I further informed Judge Griesa of my intention to have him disqualified.

My new complaint was assigned to Judge Charles Stewart. But after Griesa had received my letter, he surreptitiously took away from Judge Stewart the new matter I brought and dismissed it, claiming that it contained substantially the same material as the first matter. Judge Stewart aided Judge Griesa in accomplishing this purpose by lulling me into believing that he still had the complaint.

Judge Griesa's surprise decision, dated February 2, 1983, read "Both of these captioned actions are dismissed...the dismissal of these actions is final." I appealed Judge Griesa's decision to the Federal Court of Appeals.

The judges of the Federal Court of Appeals did not respond appreciatively to my appeal, which said, "Just how much contact and what transpired between Judge Griesa and Judge Stewart. Why and what initiated this transfer, without notice are questions deserving of answers."

I was not to get answers. Lawyers do not tell how they cheat clients, and judges do not reveal the methods they use to cheat lawyers. The clandestine and devious methods of the judiciary are not for public view.

Judge Griesa had a job to do. He did it. His decision concluded the opposite of what it should have concluded. Without any reason to support his conclusion, Judge Griesa summarized, "It is evident upon analysis that the complaint fails to state any valid claim recognizable in the Federal Court."

I had perfectly valid claims; I had cases and laws to support my claims. Griesa had a simple solution for my cases, my laws, and my rights. Griesa's solution was simply to deny justice—just say "denied." And in view of my talk about commissions to investigate judges, my appeals were assured of denial.

I brought four actions in the Federal courts; all were doomed.

One of my actions asked the Federal courts to order the Comptroller of the Currency to investigate the Scarsdale National Bank. In support of this request, I presented the Federal courts with the appropriate laws as they applied to national banks.

Richard A. Simpson, the United States Attorney representing the Comptroller of the Currency, did not respond in time to the legal papers I submitted, which were now before Judge Robert Carter. As a result, it was necessary for Simpson to obtain Judge Carter's permission to file his papers. In order to get this permission, however, he had to make his request by September 8, 1982; he did not. He was late; it was already September 16, 1982. To accomplish his purpose,

Simpson backdated his papers to read September 7, 1982. Simpson had simply filed a false affidavit.

These unethical practices of the Assistant United States Attorney led to Judge Carter's decision to dismiss my complaint.

It was not the first time I had been subjected to the misuse of power by Federal and state prosecutors. Ira Block, a high-ranking United States Attorney, had already demonstrated this power, when he arbitrarily refused to investigate the charges I made against Scarsdale National Bank, though he knew that crimes had been committed by that bank. So too did Assistant District Attorney Kenneth Citarella of Westchester County, who at first wanted to investigate the activities of Scarsdale National Bank, but abruptly changed his mind after discussing the matter with his superior, District Attorney Carl Vergari. I pleaded to Citarella:

> *Yalkowsky: There is no crime regarding Scarsdale National Bank? That forged checks are not a crime, is that what you are saying?*

> *Citarella: What we are saying is that based upon the material that you have given to us we see insufficient evidence for us to proceed.*

> *Yalkowsky: You've seen the checks? You've seen the erasures of names of Scarsdale Bank, you know, Eastchester Bank inserted to its place and you don't see that as a crime?*

> *Citarella: No.*

Kenneth Citarella and Ira Block, like most members of government agencies, commissions, and judicial bodies, did not take long to realize that the powerful men and organizations they were charged to oversee could do a great deal more good for them than the irritating victims of injustice they were sworn to protect. Once that calculation had been made, performance of their official duties became a seldom given gift, rather than a guaranteed right.

Simpson finally responded to my charge of his having submitted numerous late, backdated affidavits by explaining to the Federal Court of Appeals justices that his papers were "timely filed." Simpson lied directly to the court. His papers were late and void, and filed late and void. The Federal Court records confirmed this and the judges of the Federal Court of Appeals knew this. I awaited the day I could appear before the Court of Appeals judges and call Simpson's misconduct to their attention.

In May of 1983 I learned that my appeal to the Federal Court of Appeals would be heard on July 11. I thought that in the meantime I could have long-overdue surgery performed, with enough time to convalesce and be able to appear in court on the scheduled date. I entered the hospital and was operated upon on May 25, 1983.

A certain Federal judge, however, upon learning of my illness, anonymously rescheduled the date of my court appearance for a month earlier, at a time I could not appear. I asked for an adjournment. My request was so reasonable that even the lawyers in opposition to me did not object. But they were not the ones who changed the date. It was that particular judge's very own idea, conceived by him before I even knew who he was.

I would also learn later that this same judge was responsible for other strange anonymous decisions rendered in my disfavor. I finally learned who he was—Ellsworth Van Graafieland, who would be the presiding judge hearing my case in the Court of Appeals.

I could not possibly appear in the Federal court on June 13, 1983, the date Van Graafieland scheduled. I could not even walk at that time.

Peree, however, did appear in my place. I gave her a typewritten statement to read to the court, a statement that contained the arguments I would have presented had I been well enough to be there.

Van Graafieland, who was opposed to Peree reading my statement, reluctantly agreed to let her speak—but only for five minutes; the statement could not be read in less than fifteen minutes. Peree told me she read it as fast as she could but doubted that anyone could have understood what she said at the speed she was reading. She described how Van Graafieland's face opened into a condescending smile when she finished. The other lawyers scampered to say something in rebuttal, but Judge Van Graafieland waved them off. He did not think it necessary for them to respond. The lawyers were all smiling—they huddled and congratulated each other again.

Van Graafieland's decisions came quickly. Four days later, on June 17, 1983, he dismissed the three matters I had appealed before him.

Fair Warning

On July 7, 1983, I complained of the misconduct of Judges Thomas Griesa and Ellsworth Van Graafieland to Chief Justice Wilfred Feinberg of the Federal Court of Appeals. The Court of Appeals had a section devoted to complaints made against judges. Judge Feinberg was the judge in charge of that section.

A month later, Feinberg rendered his decision; it was done in a style I had seen many times before. He recited my complaints, and followed his recitation by concluding that my complaints were unsubstantiated.

The purpose of Judge Feinberg's recitation of my charges was to show how carefully the Federal Court recognized and evaluated charges brought against a judge. Feinberg then followed his recitation by dismissing my charges, contemptuously labeling each of them as being either baseless, frivolous, or completely unsupported. His decision, coming from a judge and court of reverential esteem, presented an impregnable document of credibility and authenticity. Of the many methods of judicial dishonesty, repeating charges and then dismissing them is one of the most insidious and efficacious. It carries with it a note of scornful ridicule of the charges, as well as the rectitude of the official decision; especially when it is rendered by an eminent jurist or respected institution. Examples of this process abound.

Judge Wilfred Feinberg's predecessor, Judge Irving Kaufman, in opposing Federal legislation to create a special panel to watch over suspected corrupt Federal Court judges, concluded that there was no corruption in the Southern District of the Federal Court. Judge Kaufman reached that conclusion after his "own investigation," despite persuasive evidence presented to him that should have resulted in his reaching the opposite conclusion.

The special panel, headed by the prestigious law firm of Paul, Weiss, Rifkind that investigated New York City Chief Medical Examiner Elliot Gross, who was charged with producing misleading autopsy reports, used this same method. It found that, although Doctor Gross switched samples of body tissue from the deceased author Tennessee Williams with body tissue of another deceased, Dr. Gross could not "fairly be faulted for his cautious and discreet handling of the Williams' specimens."

After reciting the charges brought against Judge Louis Grossman of his having threatened a four-year-old boy with jail and handcuffs, the New York State Judicial Conduct Commission concluded that Judge Grossman was not motivated by vindictiveness.

The same Judicial Conduct Commission also determined that Judge Frank Vaccaro, who had received gifts from a law firm in exchange for his favorable rulings, had merely displayed "injudicious and improper" behavior. They concluded that there was no evidence Judge Vaccaro accepted bribes. The Commission reached this conclusion, notwithstanding indisputable evidence that the law firm provided Vaccaro with

a weekend stay at the Kutcher's Country Club, a stereo speaker, a diamond and emerald ring, and payment of other bills of the judge...

Again and again, judges, commissions, and investigating bodies, in the interests of political expediency, have made conclusions that were the exact opposite of what they should have been.

On August 22, 1983, I formally and legally responded to Judge Feinberg's dismissal of my charges. In my response I accused Judge Feinberg of being a common liar. The evidence was there; I provided it.

Judge Feinberg did not know how to react. The highest judge of the Southern District of the Federal Court lost control of himself. The same day he received my letter, he personally called the FBI.

Within hours, an FBI agent, John Doorley, called me. Doorley wanted to know if or why I was threatening Judge Feinberg. He read to me over the phone the note that Feinberg claimed I had written to him. It read:

> I am going to give you, Judge Feinberg, fair warning, I gave similar fair warning to Judge Milton Mollen and to some other wonderful judges performing in our State and Federal Courts, and that fair warning to you, Judge Feinberg, is that I do not proceed empty-handed.

Doorley said to me, "What I would like to do is just come over and straighten the whole thing out before it goes any further."

Doorley had read only one paragraph of my letter; I asked him to read the rest of it so that he could see that what I had written was obviously not a threat. Doorley said that he was only given the one paragraph. I explained to Doorley that there was a full letter and that what he had read to me was taken out of context. I then read the rest of the letter over the phone to Doorley—it was a three-page document. The letter explained that I was not proceeding empty-handed but had evidence to support my charges—evidence that included tape recordings and documents.

FBI agent Doorley was sincerely amazed that he had been provided with only a small portion of my letter. He confessed to not seeing any further reason for him to continue his inquiry, but he still wanted to be sure and check with his superior. Doorley called me back with his new instructions. He and his partner were ordered to come to my home. Doorley said, "Southern District has requested I just come up and talk to you, we're on our way."

When Doorley arrived, I told him that I had complained of vast corruption for years and could not speak to an agent, but one call from Judge Feinberg and two FBI agents were at my door. Doorley admitted to me that, indeed, it was true that his visit was pursuant to the insistent direction of Justice Wilfred Feinberg.

The visit was purposeless.

Doorley and his co-agent left my home without fully understanding why they were there in the first place. Empty phrases, smiles, and handshakes were all a part of the visit. The final comment was that I would be notified as to whether or not Judge Feinberg would be bringing charges against me. Feinberg wanted me to know that his power, the power to send two FBI men to my home, was only a preview of what I might expect to happen to me if I continued to make further allegations of corruption in his court.

Writs of Certiorari

In late September of 1983 I appealed all three of Van Graafieland's decisions to the United States Supreme Court.

I had to follow the judicial process to its last stop. Had I not appealed all the way to the United States Supreme Court, it could be argued that I had not given the process a full opportunity to correct itself. Within days my appeals, called petitions for writs of certiorari, were denied without a word of comment.

The "writ of certiorari" is the legal, authentic-sounding Latin term used to describe the arbitrary and cruel power the United States Supreme Court possesses: to pick and choose, as it sees fit, which injustices it will address and which injustices it will ignore.

Not only the highest courts ignore cases brought before them. This immoral, cruel performance of judicial duties occurs in all our courts. The State Supreme Court judges often do not read cases brought before them, nor do the Federal Court judges. Federal Judge Thomas Griesa openly and brazenly admitted that he did not read the case I had presented to him.

Ancient Egyptian literature, in explaining the goals of justice, insisted that the dispensers of justice were not merely to wait until called upon to perform their duties, but instead were required to look aggressively for cases demanding their attention and seek to correct injustice wherever it could be found.

The high qualities required of judges of ancient times, however, did not survive. What did survive were every means to protect judges and clothe them with respectability, while permitting them to do as they wish. Judge Edward Greenfield, in dismissing my charges against Judge Walsh, quoted the prevalent law of our day when he ruled:

> *A judge is immune from civil liability for all acts performed within his judicial capacity...even if such actions are in excess of the judge's jurisdiction and are alleged to have been done maliciously or corruptly.*

On November 17, 1983, the Federal Court of Appeals dismissed my remaining action against the Comptroller of the Currency and the United States Attorney's office. They would not punish Scarsdale National Bank, nor admonish the United States Attorney Richard Simpson, no matter how compelling my arguments were.

I decided to go no further. My voyage in the Federal courts was over.

Ancient Times

While I had no intention of ever again appearing in the Federal courts, I still had some unfinished business remaining in the state courts.

After the $50,000 which Walsh awarded to Shedler, Weiss, and Kozupsky was taken from my accounts, I appealed Walsh's decision. I claimed that the decision was wrong because Deana had assets.

Late in 1983 I appeared in the Appellate Division, Second Department, to argue my appeal orally. There was, in fact, nothing to argue. Deana was not destitute; the lawyers had been paid. It was a fraud, and the judges I appeared before were part of the fraud. Instead of repeating what they had seen and heard so many time before, I decided to tell the judges a respected and verified ancient Egyptian story that happened over 3,000 years ago in the city of Thebes.

It was about a court case, the case of Peser, a civic-minded high government official, and the charges he brought against Pewero, the Superintendent of Police, concerning the manner in which the investigation of the robberies of the ten tombs of the great Pharaohs was conducted.

The judges assigned to listen to my appeal appeared uneasy. Apparently, they thought it odd for me to use the few precious moments I had to discuss with them a matter that could not be found in any law book. One of the judges, Guy Mangano, was smiling; he seemed to think that perhaps the strain of the litigation had finally taken its toll on me.

I continued relating the ancient story, telling how, when Peser learned that eight thieves had successfully burglarized the royal tombs of the Pharaohs, he reported what he had learned to Khamwese, the Governor, without realizing that in so doing he was not merely questioning the integrity of the Superintendent of Police, but was also questioning the integrity of the Governor, since, as most Egyptologists have concluded, the Governor and the Chief of Police were all the while sharing in the proceeds of the burglaries.

A Commission of Inquiry was appointed by Governor Khamwese. Archaeologists have recovered and preserved for us the Commission's report, which was compiled in the sixteenth year of Pharaoh Ramses IX's reign. It read,

> *Pyramids of the royal ancestors, examined this day by the inspectors:*
>
> *found uninjured pyramids—9*
> *found broken-into pyramids—1*
> Total—10

The Commission disputed Peser's claims, finding them highly exaggerated. According to the Commissioners only one tomb was broken into, not ten as Peser had claimed. Jubilantly, the civil servants of Thebes, connected with protecting the tombs, organized a parade to celebrate their victory over Peser. They marched in a procession right to his private residence, where they jeeringly proclaimed their happiness at the Commission's findings and their distaste for the charges he had made.

Peser, hurt by the insulting conduct of the mob, angrily promised that a great deal more evidence was forthcoming to substantiate his claims. Peser also called the Commission findings a farce and vowed to notify Pharaoh himself. Pewero, the manipulative Superintendent of Police, upon learning of Peser's vow, immediately informed Governor Khamwese of Peser's intentions. The Governor was so worried by the doubts that could be cast upon his administration if Peser's charges were believed by Pharaoh that he had the case immediately recalled. Three of the eight men who admitted to robbing the ten tombs were brought before him.

Governor Khamwese personally introduced the evidence. He explained to the court that he had made the inspections and reached his findings from personal knowledge. He said only one of the royal tombs had been broken into, not ten as claimed by Peser. The three thieves, unwilling to contradict Governor Khamwese, no matter what they had already told Peser, testified just as the Governor desired.

Peser attended the hearing and heard his witnesses recant their testimony before his very eyes and claim that they never entered the tombs they previously had admitted entering. The Commission of Inquiry hearing turned out to be a public denunciation of Peser. Peser was totally defeated. His name was never seen again.

The evidence modern Egyptologists and archaeologists have uncovered tends to confirm the truth of Peser's claims—he had been unjustly denounced. Archaeological evidence verified that ten tombs had indeed been robbed by the men Peser accused in the sixteenth year of Ramses IX's reign, just as he had said all along.

The judges sitting were justices Guy Mangano, Moses Weinstein, Frank O'Connor, and Richard Brown. They wore bemused expressions on their faces while they listened to my lecture on ancient Egypt. Their faces, however, turned stonily expressionless once they recognized I was discussing with them a matter they had hoped would be forever erased from their memories—Special Prosecutor Maurice Nadjari's tribulations with Governor Hugh Carey concerning the charges Nadjari brought against Bronx Democratic Leader Patrick Cunningham and the indictments he brought against ten influential and high-ranking New York State judges.

Looking back at that period: Governor Hugh Carey was openly disappointed when Maurice Nadjari was permitted to remain in office an additional six months, especially after the Special Prosecutor had publicly stated that he was fired by Carey only because he was investigating Patrick Cunningham and several other judges who were friends of the Governor. Carey thought that Nadjari had questioned his integrity. He demanded vindication.

As a result of Governor Carey's demands, a respected jurist was sought to hear evidence and to find out why the Governor fired Maurice Nadjari: whether it was because of Carey's growing fear of Nadjari's investigations into sales of judgeships and other corruption, or merely his dissatisfaction with the Special Prosecutor's performance. It was one of the most unusual investigations ever conceived. Several lawyers refused to accept the appointment, which required that a determination be made as to just what Governor Carey's introspective motives were when he fired the Special Prosecutor. Jacob Grumet, a former judge, finally accepted the appointment, which could result in only one conclusion: the conclusion Governor Carey demanded.

In the meantime, Patrick Cunningham's lawyer, Gregory Perrin, charged in open court that Nadjari had promised the Bronx Democratic Leader leniency in exchange for "the goods on the Governor." Cunningham's lawyer used the same tactic Pewero of Thebes had used to inflame Governor Khamwese against Peser three thousand years before.

Nadjari had brought several indictments against Patrick Cunningham. Among the indictments and investigations Nadjari pursued were charges that Cunningham tried to "fix" a homicide case. Nadjari was also investigating evidence he had that Cunningham had sold several lawyers the judgeships they eventually received. In addition, Nadjari was investigating Cunningham's sales of government posts to a judge's son, his tampering with witnesses and evidence, his billing procedures in his legal practice, which made bribes appear as legal fees, and his intimidation of those who would oppose him. Each of Nadjari's indictments was dismissed.

Some four years later, when Patrick Cunningham was no longer the Bronx chairman, nor the state chairman, he was charged by the Federal Government with conspiracy to obstruct justice and with perjury.

Cunningham, in his defense, had influential people testify in his behalf—among them Judge Burton Roberts. He also coerced and cajoled key witnesses to commit perjury and tamper with physical evidence. But everything went wrong. The methods that had helped Cunningham so successfully in the past no longer helped him. Witnesses who promised to say one thing said another. A former law partner testified against him. Governor Carey, no longer his close friend, offered him no help. Charges supported by evidence far less compelling than the indictments Nadjari had brought against Patrick Cunningham years before, when the Bronx leader had been in power, were now vigorously and successfully pursued by the Federal Government.

At about the same time I was telling the Appellate Division, Second Department judges the story of Peser, Patrick Cunningham was disbarred after having been convicted and sentenced to three and a half years in prison. Nadjari, it turned out, like Peser, had been right all along.

On December 19, 1983, the Appellate Division, Second Department judges rendered their decision. They reduced Shedler and Weiss's counsel-fee award to $35,000. They thought that by returning $15,000 to me I would be sufficiently compensated. I could not accept their award.

Stealing from the Children

While my tribulations continued, the most awful of Weiss and Kozupsky's actions was brought against me in New York County—the matter of Irina Yalkowsky, Risah Yalkowsky, and Larin Yalkowsky by Deana Yalkowsky Napolitano, their mother and natural guardian, against Stanley Yalkowsky.

In December of 1981 I was served with a complaint brought on behalf of my children by my wife, claiming that I had stolen some $117,000 worth of stock from them back in 1974. Weiss and Kozupsky claimed that I had intended to give this money to my children as a gift but had not done so.

Just months after I had made a complaint to the Bar Association charging Shedler, Weiss, and Kozupsky with fraud, and just months after Allen Kozupsky vowed to ruin my relationship with my children, I was being charged by Weiss and Kozupsky with having stolen my children's money.

The suit should have been dismissed at its inception. There was no legitimate purpose for it. The reason Judge Peter J. McQuillan of the New York Supreme Court, who first heard the matter, did not dismiss it at its inception was that he was misled by the falsely sworn affidavits of Deana's lawyers, who swore under oath that "Stanley Yalkowsky admitted that he converted the funds."

It was a monstrous action without any basis; every legal principle called for its dismissal, as did every human principle; yet the Appellate Division and Court of Appeals judges encouraged the action to continue.

Ruminating on the possibility that I could expose their corruption unless they could somehow strike back at me, the Appellate Courts of New York State were willing to cast me as a thief who would steal from his own children. Of all the devices the Appellate Courts used against me, permitting this action was the most abominable.

Before the action was brought to trial, however, the matter was brought before several judges. One of them, Louis Grossman, was the judge who had been censured for having harassed and tormented a four-year-old boy after having been told that the boy had said something uncomplimentary about him.

At one of the conferences before Justice Louis Grossman, another man was seated quietly beside him. This man was later introduced to me as retired Supreme Court Justice Milton Sanders. Sanders tried coaxing me to settle, insisting that I would lose the case if I persisted. When I asked Judge Grossman who had invited ex-judge Sanders to attend my private conference in his chambers, the matter was shifted to Judge Michael Dontzin, the former aide to Mayor Lindsay, who had been investigated years before for selling judgeships.

On January 16, 1984, when the matter was brought before Judge Dontzin, Allen Weiss asked to speak to Dontzin privately. I complained that I did not think it proper for the Judge to excuse me and speak to Mr. Weiss alone. Nonetheless, Dontzin asked me to wait outside his chambers.

Just moments before his private meeting with Weiss, Dontzin chose a February date for the trial, over which he was to preside. After his private meeting with Weiss, Dontzin announced that the case would be heard in January and that a different judge would preside.

All I could do to voice my protest was to make a statement to the court stenographer. I said to him, "At our last appearance here Judge Dontzin said to leave the room. Immediately upon my returning, Judge Dontzin says that this case is going to be turned over to some out-of-state judge, this is improper and part of the same sort of thing that I have been faced with throughout this matter."

Dontzin defended, "Well, Mr. Yalkowsky, let me make clear to you my conversation with Mr. Weiss, when I asked you to leave, had nothing to do with your accusations."

I did not expect Dontzin to admit that he conducted improper deliberations with Weiss and other judges privately and without my presence. I did not expect Dontzin to admit that his decision to change the February 14th date to a January 18th date for the matter to be heard by an upstate judge was a direct result of private, judicially improper instructions he received.

Kozupsky, who was there with Weiss, then said, "I will just ask whether Mr. Yalkowsky is going to object to a judge from the Second Department."

I replied, "My objections are really actually meaningless. I can only hope for a jury."

Dontzin reassured me, "That's exactly why we are giving you one."

I appeared before the special judge chosen—Judge Lawrence Kahn. It was January 18, 1984; trial was to begin. Judge Kahn refused to allow me a jury. All Dontzin's assurances and the previous orders of the court guaranteeing me a jury trial were discarded.

Kozupsky called Larin to the witness stand.

Kozupsky questioned Larin, "There was no duress to force you to sign that retainer. I did not force you to sign it, did I?"

All Kozupsky was trying to do was establish that it was not his law firm that encouraged my children to sue me.

Kozupsky did not even attempt to present a case; Kozupsky did not want to win. But when Kozupsky put Larin on the witness stand and had Larin ostensibly testify against me, even though Larin said nothing dishonest, or detrimental to me, he left Larin tainted with the lasting pain of having testified against his father.

I asked Larin, "When did you find out about this action, Larin?"

He replied, "I found out about it recently, approximately three or four weeks ago. My mother told me about it first."

I continued, "Then who else told you about it?"

Larin answered, "Mr. Kozupsky explained the situation to me in his office about a week and a half ago."

I asked, "What did Mr. Kozupsky explain to you about the action?"

Larin replied, "It was unlawful for the accounts to be taken out once they were purchased."

I asked, "In other words, you did not know anything about it being unlawful?"

Larin replied, "No, Mr. Kozupsky said it was unlawful."

Kozupsky protested, "That was never our claim that he stole any money."

That was Kozupsky's claim, however. I asked Larin if he had read the complaint, but before Larin could answer, Kozupsky instructed Larin, "Don't answer the question." Kozupsky then pleaded with Kahn, "Your Honor, isn't it enough?"

Deana then took the witness stand. Kozupsky questioned Deana as if he were working for me. Kozupsky wanted the action dismissed, and he wanted me to know it. Kozupsky did not ask one question or receive one answer from Deana that was in any way supportive of the action.

All that Kozupsky wanted to establish was that the suit was Deana's and not his.

Kahn asked me, "All right, Mr. Yalkowsky, any questions of this witness?"

I replied, "I don't think so."

Several months later, Judge Kahn reached his decision. Kahn ruled that the case against me was dismissed. Kahn wrote his decision with only one objective in mind—to word it in such a way that it protected Weiss and Kozupsky and did not embarrass the Court of Appeals and Appellate Division judges who used this suit as a weapon of vengeance against me.

* * *

On March 5, 1984, Michael Gentile, the chief counsel of the Departmental Disciplinary Committee announced that my complaint against Kenneth Horwitz was dismissed. On the same date he also dismissed the Disciplinary Committee complaint Justice Milton Mollen brought against me.

The members of the Departmental Disciplinary Committee considered this a wonderful act of diplomacy; they hoped I would be placated by this act of benevolence. They would dismiss my legitimate complaint and balance that dismissal by discharging Justice Milton Mollen's worthless complaint against me. It did not matter to them that Mollen's complaint against me contained no intelligible charge other than his disapproval of my claims of his court's corruption, nor did it matter to them that I had incontrovertible evidence of Kenneth Horwitz's misconduct.

Eight Dell Road

In January of 1985 Peree married Brendan O'Keefe. Deana, the other children, and I attended the wedding. I did not speak to Deana; I had not spoken to her since the divorce. A few days after the wedding, I decided to give Deana the house on Dell Road. The house was the most valuable asset I still possessed. What I was doing seemed to make no sense.

I thought I gave Deana the house to express how deeply I appreciated her for what she had done for me. But when I decided to give Deana the house, the reason I did so was not then in my mind; I had no reason. It was a spontaneous act. The reasons and explanation came later, to make what I did at least sound rational. This is the reason I preferred, but I really do not know why I gave Deana the house.

I am no longer so certain of my reasons or the cause-effect sequence; at one time I was. I now see cause and effect as one unit. I had in the past believed that "because" explained or was the cause of "why." I now believe that cause is no more responsible for effect than night is responsible for day.

My view of the world is just one picture. It is as if everything is a circle that prevents us from seeing around the bend. But if we flatten the bend, all is then in our view, just like the pages of a book that have not yet been turned or the frames of a movie reel that have not been reached.

In May of 1985 the Departmental Disciplinary Committee dismissed my charges against Richard Friedman. Forging a check and stealing over $10,000 from me they did not consider misconduct.

In that same month I also learned that Bert Subin had

arranged, with the help of Judge Michael Dontzin, to embezzle $100,000 from me. Bert Subin, my friend for so many years, assured of the protection of the Departmental Disciplinary Committee and certain that I was of no use to him any longer, decided to steal from me every penny he could.

Subin and Edelman

Many years before Subin had made this decision, he had represented me in a dispute I had with a lawyer, Jerome Edelman. The dispute was over the question of whether Edelman or I would be entitled to the legal fees received in behalf of a client who was seriously injured in an automobile accident.

I had been that particular client's lawyer for some time before I was approached by Edelman, who told me that it would be better that he handle the matter, since he had very close connections with the insurance company I was suing. The insurance company adjuster called me to confirm this relationship. Edelman guaranteed me a fantastic settlement recovery. As a further inducement he offered me 60 percent of the attorney's fees; I was persuaded to allow him to share in my fee.

Later, however, Edelman advised me that he needed extra money on the case for judge's expenses. When I did not respond to his request, he warned me that unless I agreed to take a smaller percentage of the fee he would have to "do something to protect" himself.

I did not, at first, understand what Edelman meant by doing "something to protect" himself. The explanation soon came. Within days I received a startling note from my client. It said, "I want Jerome Edelman to be my lawyer."

In 1979, Subin, representing me, served a complaint upon Edelman. The complaint stated that Edelman interfered with the contractual relationship I had with my client.

But then in November of 1981 Subin learned about the letter I had written to the judges of the State of New York—the Stern letter—that detailed corruption in the courts. Subin knew where his allegiance lay. Our years of friendship were over. I became his instant and despised enemy.

By mid-1982, once it was clear to Subin that I was powerless to defend myself and no threat to him or the courts, he began his assault. He stopped sending me the fees I was entitled to for the many cases I had referred to him over the years.

Try as I did, I could not speak to Subin, who assigned Maria Donadio, his secretary, to fend off my calls. Maria would no longer tell me whether any of my cases were settled. She would no longer tell me what cases I had pending. She refused to let me know what moneys were due me. She told me she was under specific instructions from Bert Subin not to give me any information.

It was not until May of 1985, nearly three years later, that I again heard from Bert Subin. I received a call from his secretary. I was told that I must be in court the next morning or my case against Jerome Edelman would be dismissed.

On May 10, I met with Subin, who told me that he thought my case against Edelman was worthless. Later that morning we appeared before Judge Ethel Danzig, who also told me that she thought the case was worthless.

Judge Ethel Danzig had a very good reason to feel as she did. She was herself mired in a similar controversy. Her husband, Stanley Danzig, had been accused by his former partners of secretly misappropriating $250,000 and refusing to return the money. This conduct resulted in the partners severing their relationship with him. Judge Ethel Danzig as a result, it was charged, orchestrated a raid, which involved her husband and five others breaking into the law firm's office in the late evening and taking legal documents. Judge Danzig was also accused of having warned her husband's former law partners of "big trouble" if they didn't watch themselves. Judge Edward Greenfield, always ready to help a fellow judge, sealed many of the records of Judge Danzig's participation in the matter, including a note written by her that instructed her husband to "take" the files that belonged to her.

I was suing Edelman for stealing a case from me; my lawyer, I later learned, had stolen cases from me; and I was appearing before a judge who was accused of aiding in stealing cases from other lawyers while she was a sitting judge. Judge Danzig thought it best to refer the matter elsewhere. The matter turned up in the hands of Judge Robert White, who ruled against me.

I appealed his decision. A year later, the Appellate Division, First Department, endorsed as acceptable the conduct of Jerome Edelman. I appealed further, to the Court of Appeals. In a sworn affidavit I informed the Court of Appeals judges that Jerome Edelman admitted that his prime reason for refusing to honor his contract with me was his need to get a greater portion of the fee so that he could pay judges who insisted upon receiving a share in his recoveries. The judges of the Court of Appeals ignored my sworn statements, and dismissed my appeal.

The Diaz Case

That same May 10, 1985 day that I appeared before Judge Ethel Danzig gave me the first opportunity I had in years to ask Subin about the many cases I had remaining with him. I asked Subin about the case of Pablo Diaz. Subin told me the case had been dismissed. But when I visited the clerk's office and looked up the case of Pablo Diaz, I learned that the case in fact had not been dismissed. Subin had settled the case for $600,000 and was in the process of stealing over $100,000 in fees from me.

Looking over the Diaz file, I found a startling document. Subin declared that he did not represent Myrna Diaz, Pablo's wife. Not only did Subin deny he represented Myrna Diaz, he also abused her in his writings with vicious slanders. Subin charged Myrna Diaz with leaving her husband Pablo because he was a cripple.

Although Myrna Diaz could not understand Subin's purpose, when I read the document I could. In 1976 Bert Subin brought an action in behalf of Pablo and Myrna Diaz that resulted in a recovery to them of $175,000. I was the referring lawyer and received a substantial fee as my share. That was only part of the case, however. There was still another portion of the case that remained unresolved—against a party named Thomas McCalmont, who had been driving while intoxicated. I was entitled to an even more substantial fee as my share of that section of the matter.

Subin reasoned that if he could establish that the case I referred to him was already settled and that he alone was rehired by Pablo Diaz in 1979, he would be able to disavow his obligation to pay a legal fee to Myrna Diaz and a referral fee to me. To succeed in this ruse, which would make Subin a great deal more money,

232

since on this occasion $600,000 was collected, Subin had
to claim that he had nothing to do with Myrna Diaz after
her strife with her husband began, and also did not know
in 1976, when he first started the suit, that Thomas
McCalmont had been intoxicated.

Subin, however, had always known that McCalmont had
been intoxicated. The court records showed that Subin
had specifically charged McCalmont with being
intoxicated in his complaint of 1976. In that complaint
Subin alleged that "at the time and place of the
accident, the defendant, Thomas McCalmont, was
intoxicated." Yet on January 11, 1985, Subin swore in
front of Judge Michael Dontzin that when he was retained
by Myrna Diaz in 1976, "it was not known that the
driver, Thomas McCalmont had been drinking."

Subin's dealings with Myrna Diaz were not limited to
falsely claiming that he did not represent her and that
he did not know Thomas McCalmont was intoxicated; Subin
had other means of defrauding Myrna Diaz: in addition to
forging checks, Subin also received interest on monies
to which he had no lawful right. All this was known to
Judge Dontzin, who was asked by Myrna Diaz:

> I do not understand why attorney Subin has
> not produced actual releases, copy of deposit
> slips, original bankbooks and matter like this
> to prove his point. Since attorney Subin is so
> aware of interest, I would be interested in his
> accounting of the exact day he was paid the
> $175,000, where the money was put to collect
> interest and who was given the interest on the
> money?

Judge Dontzin made certain that nothing could be
learned of Subin's fraud. And then to make doubly certain that Subin and he had no further trouble from Myrna
Diaz, Dontzin had the ultimate solution: he arranged to

have Subin hand over to Myrna Diaz $40,000 in the form of an award. Giving Myrna Diaz that money enabled Subin to avoid answering the difficult questions she asked, and concluded the case.

Judge William Brennan

At last, in late 1985, the judges of the higher courts of this state were met with the most serious threat to their power to prevent investigation and prosecution of corrupt New York City judges that they had ever faced: New York State Supreme Court Justice William Brennan was charged with accepting bribes.

Judge Brennan's activities first came to the attention of the Nassau County District Attorney's office in 1980 when it learned that he had received substantial sums of money—$10,000 and $15,000 at a time—in exchange for his rulings that dropped serious charges brought against criminals appearing before him in the Queens Supreme Court. But it was not until four years later that Judge Brennan was finally placed under serious investigation, and then only after his criminal conduct became known to the Queens District Attorney's office, who referred the matter to the United States Attorney General's office. By then too many government agencies knew of Judge Brennan's activities. Brennan had to be arrested.

Judge Brennan's corruption was so widespread that it was impossible to investigate fully. Brennan had been a Supreme Court justice for fifteen years and accepting bribes for fifteen years—he had handled literally thousands of cases. Judge Brennan was so secure in his ability to fix cases that he promised to return whatever money he received unless he delivered the results he guaranteed.

At his trial, Judge Brennan received the enthusiastic support of several Supreme Court justices. Justice Francis X. Smith, the Administrative Judge of Queens County, described Brennan as "one of the finest Judges" he had ever known.

Judge Brennan was convicted of twenty-six counts of receiving bribes, attempted extortion, fraud, and racketeering. Yet Judge Jack B. Weinstein sentenced him to a mere five-year term, when five thousand years could not make up for the crimes Brennan had committed and allowed to be committed. The number of innocent victims who suffered because of Judge Brennan's release of guilty criminals upon the public can never be counted, nor can the damage Judge Brennan did to the morale of police officers, who risked their lives to arrest the many criminals he set free, ever be calculated.

Meanwhile, in the Illinois courts where widespread corruption was being exposed, convicted judges were sentenced to ten- and fifteen-year terms. The Chicago judges were ready to turn against each other to reduce their sentences. Federal Judge Jack Weinstein made certain, by the leniency of the sentence he imposed on Judge Brennan, that New York City judges would not be persuaded to implicate one another. Judge Brennan would serve only twenty-six months in prison: one month for each of his crimes. Judge Weinstein, in so using his discretion, prevented exposure of the massive corruption existing in the New York City courts.

In February of 1986, only days after Judge Brennan was sentenced, Judge Vito J. Titone, who had recently been appointed Justice of the Court of Appeals, solemnly announced that he, too, was being investigated for accepting bribes.

A lawyer, Martin Light, claimed that he had bribed Titone, during the time Titone was sitting as an Appellate Division judge in Brooklyn. Titone denied Light's charges, explaining that Light may have given him some small presents at Christmas time, but none that he could recall.

The matter was referred to Charles T. Hynes, the Special Prosecutor investigating corruption in the criminal justice system. Hynes, recognizing that the State of New York could not possibly permit a full-scale investigation of Judge Vito Titone while the case of Judge William Brennan was so fresh in the public's mind, went so far as to discount and ignore documentary evidence and admissions made by Judge Titone that he did in fact receive gratuities from Martin Light when he was sitting as a judge in the Appellate Division, Second Department. Hynes declared, "Each incident has been exhaustively examined...The judge's actions were not inappropriate, and there is no evidence to corroborate the allegations that were made. The matter is therefore closed." The Special Prosecutor simply reached a conclusion that contradicted the facts.

Martin Light was not the first lawyer who, after accusing a judge of accepting bribes, found himself disbarred, disgraced, or jailed, while the accused judge was entrenched even more securely. There were many others.

Another lawyer, Spencer Lader, who was serving a jail term after pleading guilty to fraud, testified under oath before a New York State Senate committee about the extensive corruption of Brooklyn and New York City judges. To support his claims, he had tape recordings and canceled checks he had paid to judges that he presented to the Committee. He also provided extremely useful information to Federal prosecutors in the hope of receiving an early release from jail. Somehow, despite the information he provided, his jail term was not shortened. Lader appealed to the Appellate Division for his release on probation.

The Appellate Division determined in mid-1985 that Lader "had breached his agreement to cooperate fully" and had "intentionally provided false, misleading and incomplete information" about criminal investigations. The Appellate Division judges reached this conclusion despite the United States Attorney General's sworn claim that Spencer Lader had provided them with "substantial information" that "proved to be truthful" and that he "fully cooperated" as a witness in a murder prosecution that resulted in a conviction.

The Years Were Flying By

Though I was still a lawyer, I could never again represent a client before the courts. The only matters I could bring to the courts were those matters where I alone was the aggrieved—and, when I did, I was not only unjustly defeated, but was vengefully set upon with scorn, scowls, and contempt by every judge in every court before which I appeared.

One judge's law clerk tried to lure me into having a fist fight with him by physically trying to stop me from leaving his office. I carefully avoided this encounter, knowing full well that a summoned court officer would most certainly have been instructed to attack me. The Appellate Division judges went further; they permitted a law firm to harass and illegally sue me for eviction from my apartment, based on false allegations brought by a corporation that did not own the building.

The years were flying by. I was a middle-aged man—a grandfather. Peree had given birth to her son, Miles. In the passing years I tried to avoid judges and lawyers as best as I could.

A matter of mine, however, still remained in the courts. I had sued a chiropractor, Burton Sheryll, for having improperly x-rayed me. In late January of 1988 the matter was ready for trial in New York City Civil Court.

Before the trial began, however, events occurred that were odd and foreboding. Two jurors curiously and abruptly asked to be relieved from the matter. Another juror volunteered that she heard something in the hall about my mental condition. That particular prospective juror was not the only one to say that she heard something negative about me in the witness area corridors. The juror sitting beside her said something similar. Though I did not understand the jurors actions, rather than postpone the trial I accepted any juror willing to sit—and challenged no one.

The trial that followed was nothing less than astonishing. Kathi Peisner, The chiropractor's lawyer, with the help of two assistants, wheeled boxes containing numerous files into the courtroom. She then proceeded to remove from these boxes legal document after legal document describing the many actions I had brought against judges over the years. "Stanley Yalkowsky sued Judge Mollen, Judge Titone, Judge Rubin. He sued federal judges, the Departmental Disciplinary Committee lawyers, banks..." Scores of judges and institutions I had sued were individually identified and named before the jury. I protested again and again. What could this possibly have to do with my case against a chiropractor?

Peisner's main thrust, from beginning to end, was to let the jurors know that I had sued judges and lawyers; going so far as to bring up, during the trial, charges I had made against Kenneth Horwitz to the Departmental Disciplinary Committee.

But how did Kathi Peisner obtain so many of these bound legal documents? None of them were subpoenaed from the court. And how did she have in her hands my legal documents that sued Michael Gentile of the Departmental Disciplinary Committee and John Keenan? Only the Disciplinary Committee and the State Attorney General lawfully possessed these documents. Besides myself and the courts nobody had them. Yet Peisner had in her possession the original documents.

Peisner also introduced into the proceedings the diagnosis of the psychiatrist, Dr. David Friedman, who, so many years before, during my matrimonial dispute, testified that my complaints against judges were evidence that I suffered from paranoia. Judge Milton Richardson, rather than restrain Peisner, encouraged her to implant the jury with the idea that anyone who sued judges had to be paranoid.

Judge Richardson knew the value of the matter before him. He knew what every judge who had been sued by me expected of him. When I offered sound legal arguments, he responded to them by telling me to "shut up." When I tried again to speak, he called for a court officer, suggesting that I could be arrested if I persisted in disobeying his commands to "shut up."

The case was not a case capable of being lost, even by the most unskilled lawyer. A chiropractor without a registered X-ray machine took illegal X-rays of me, violated a statute, and was censured, fined, and reprimanded for taking these X-rays. Nonetheless, when I tried to show that Dr. Sheryll's machine was defective by displaying documents that cited him for not having a properly functioning X-ray machine and other violations of the City Health Code, Peisner cried out that I was a liar. Judge Richardson permitted her to insult me before the jury. He permitted her to call me a liar, and encouraged the jurors to believe that I was falsely accusing Dr. Sheryll. In fact, after the trial the jurors told me that they did not look very kindly at my trying to persuade them into believing that Dr. Sheryll's X-ray machine was defective. They also let me know that they did not appreciate my having sued judges. I did not even try to correct them.

The jury ruled against me on every phase of the case. They reached their verdict on January 20, 1988, exactly ten years after Deana had told me of her adulterous affair.

Nothing will change. Even if all the judges I named

were removed, they would only be replaced by others who in a short time would be doing the very same. My only accomplishment is this recording—a depiction of human nature and civilization as it exists and has always existed.

* * *

Be assured there will be retaliation for what I have written—more intense than what I have already received. I am ready.